I0826540

Il Pleut

THIS

WORK

WAS

WRITTEN

IN

MEMORY

OF

THE

ASSASSINATED

POET

Il Pleut

A Modern Translation

Sean Fraser

Éditions des Nuages

Paris
1912

@TheatreSean

978-1-7352707-6-0

PREFACE

"The Calligrammes are an idealisation of free verse poetry and typographical precision in an era when typography is reaching a brilliant end to its career, at the dawn of the new means of reproduction that are the cinema and the phonograph."

—Guillaume Apollinaire, in a letter to André Billy

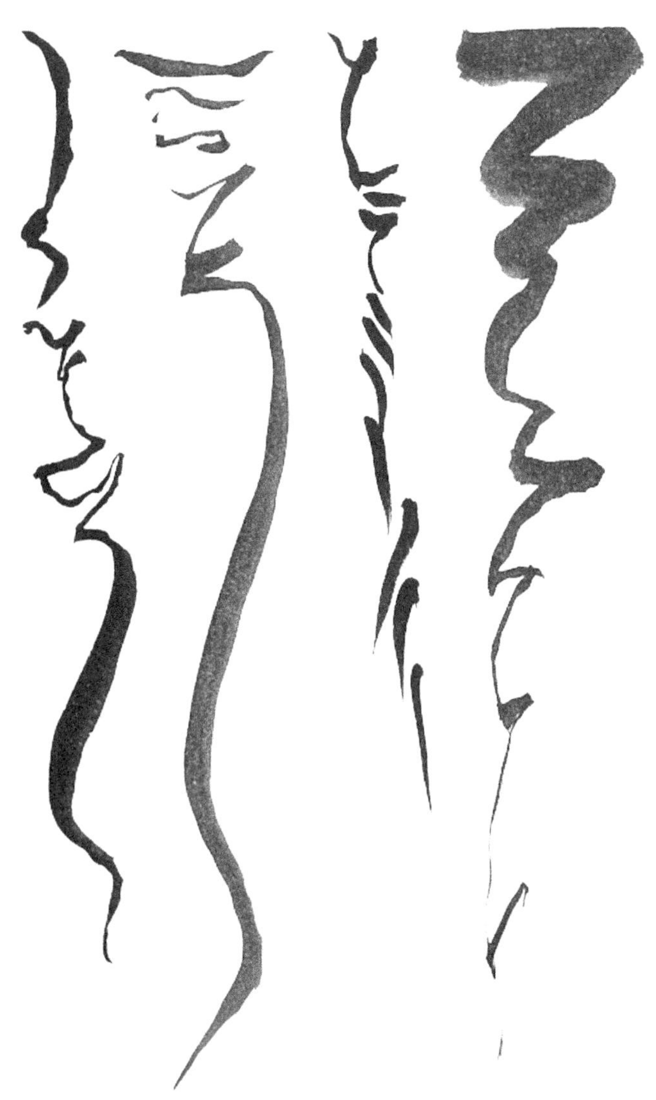

IL PLEUT

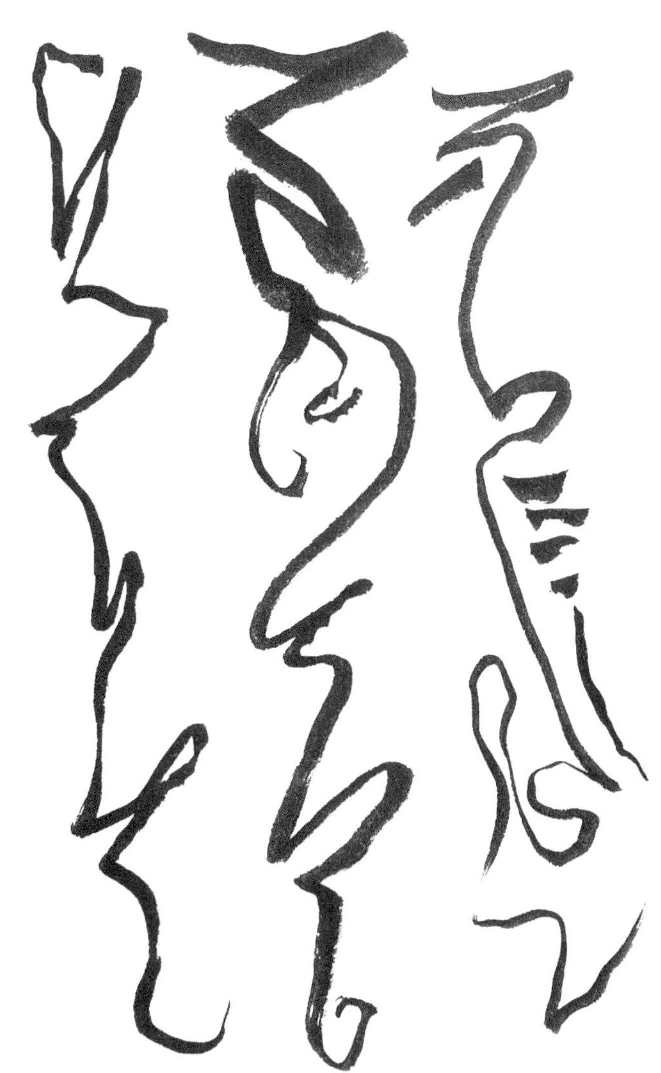

DES

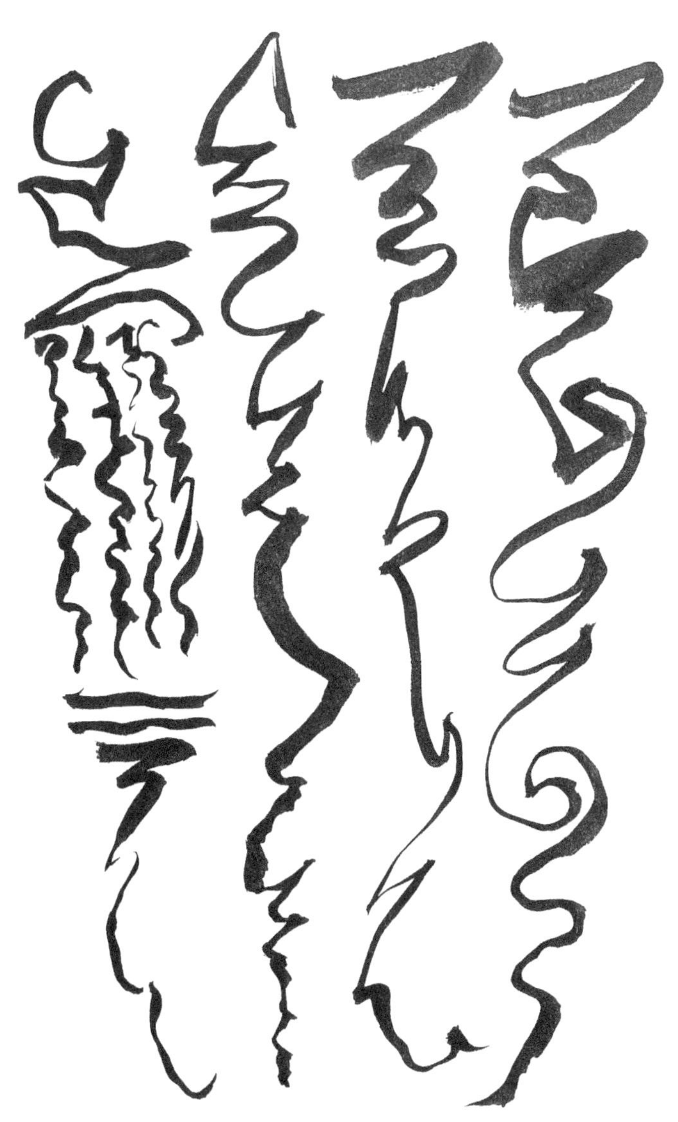

VOIX

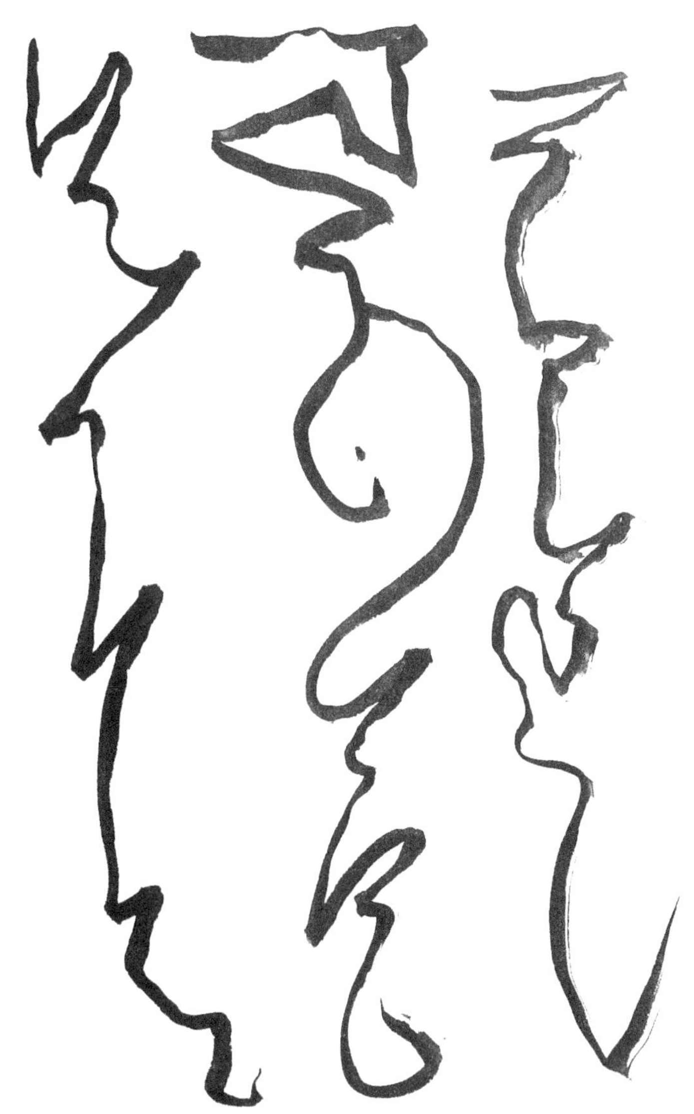

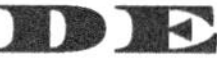

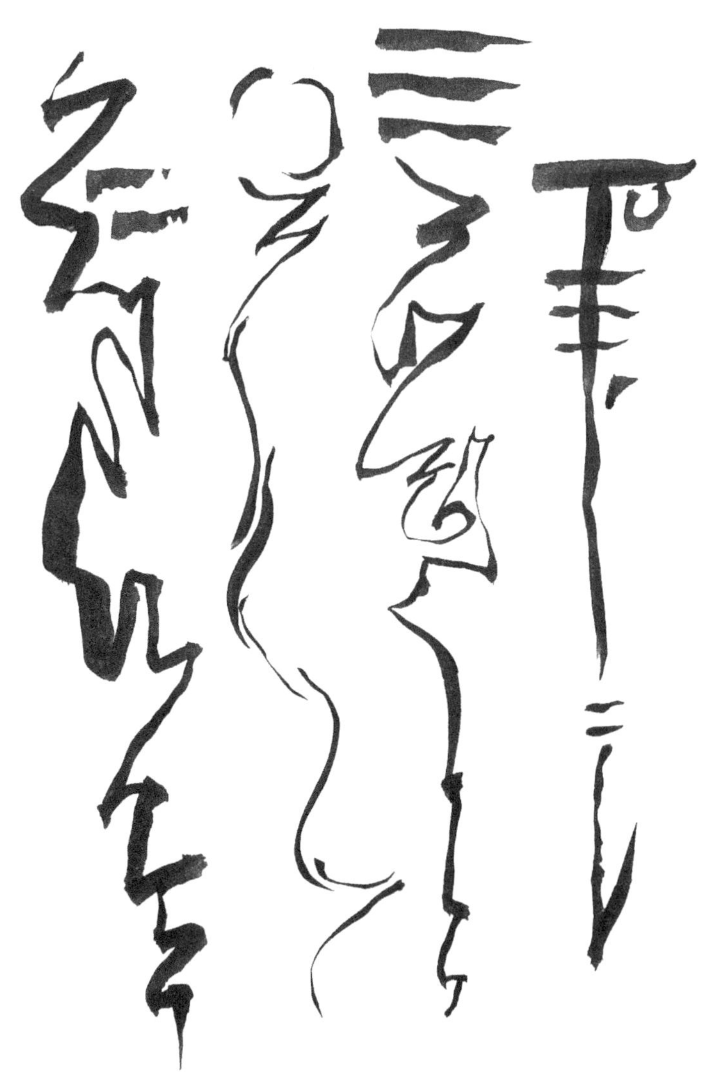

FEMMES

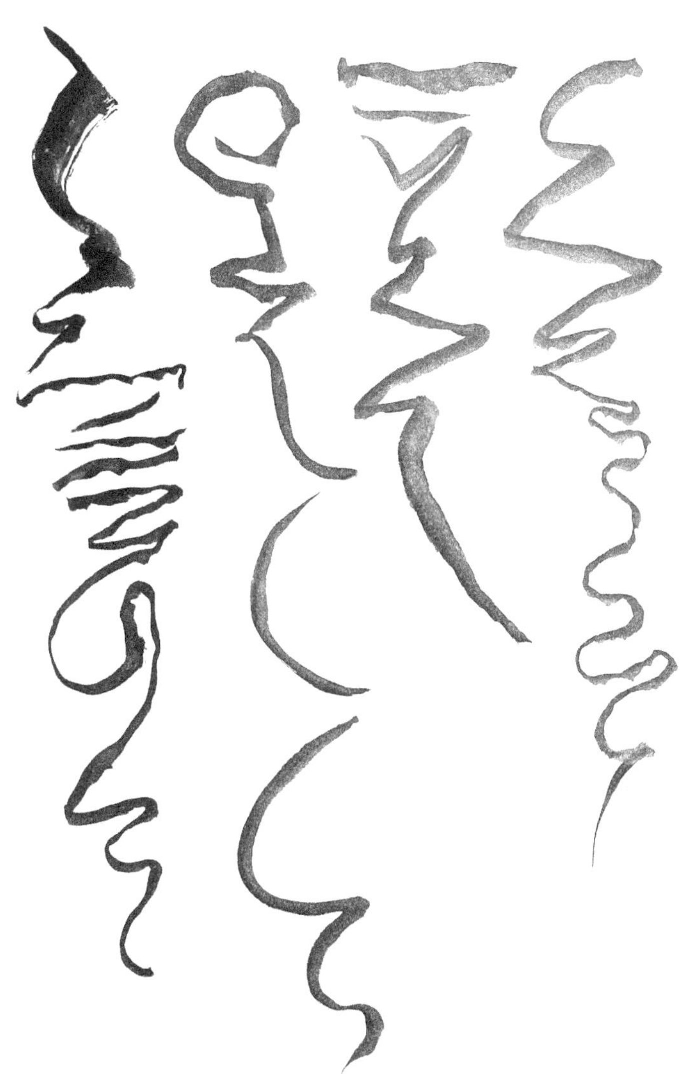

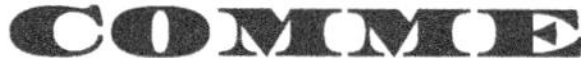

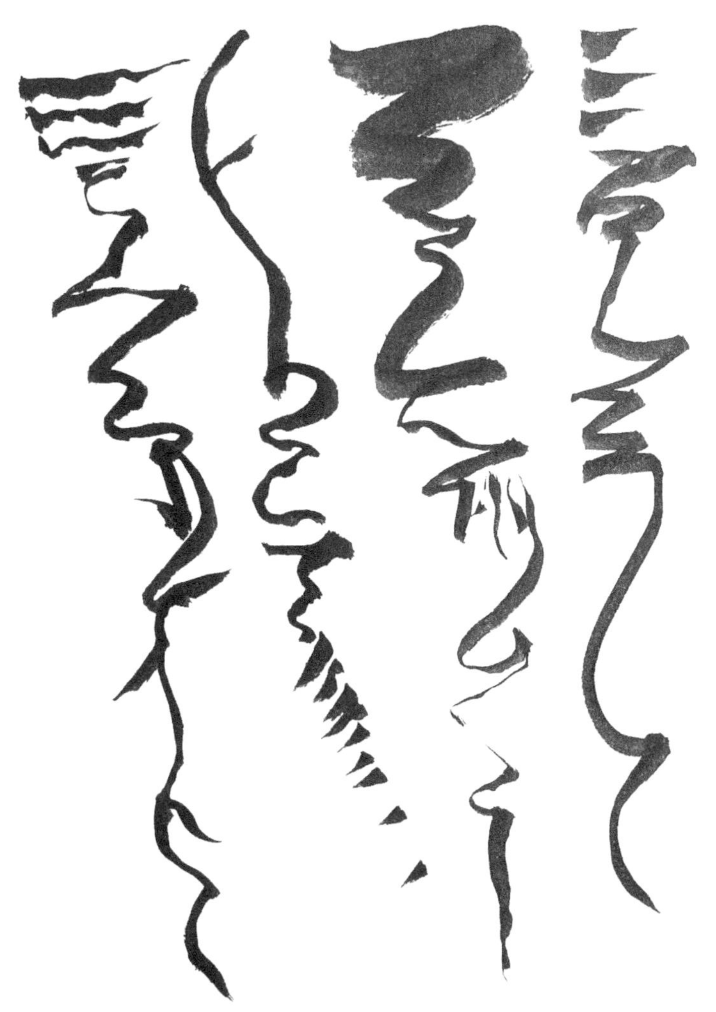

SI

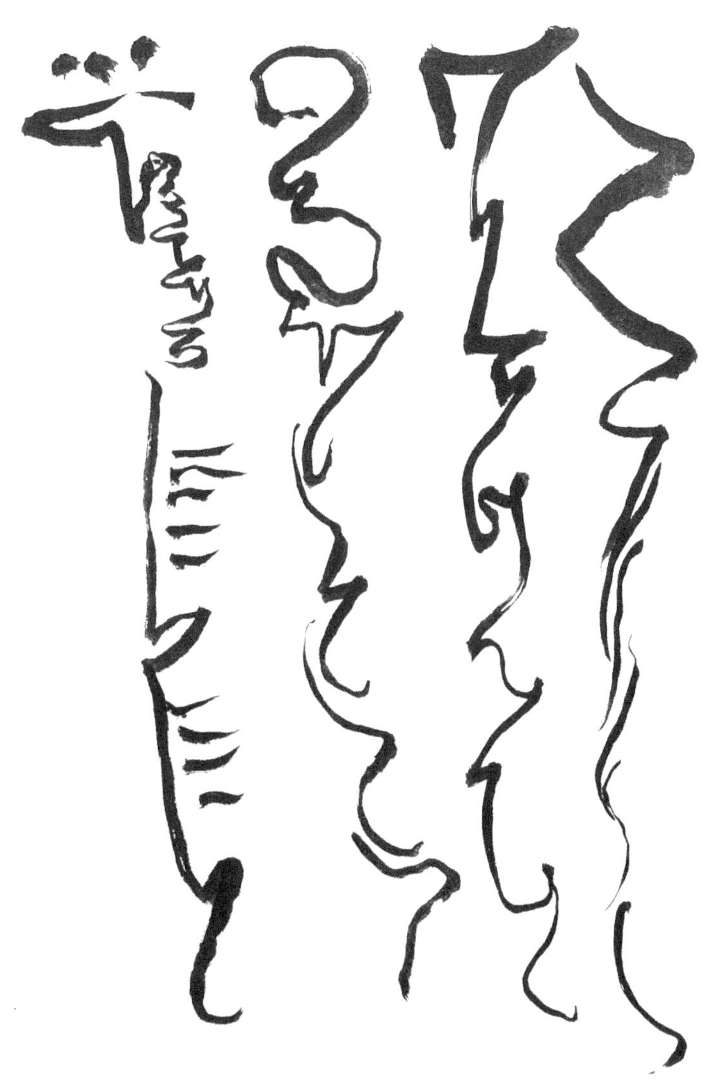

ELLES

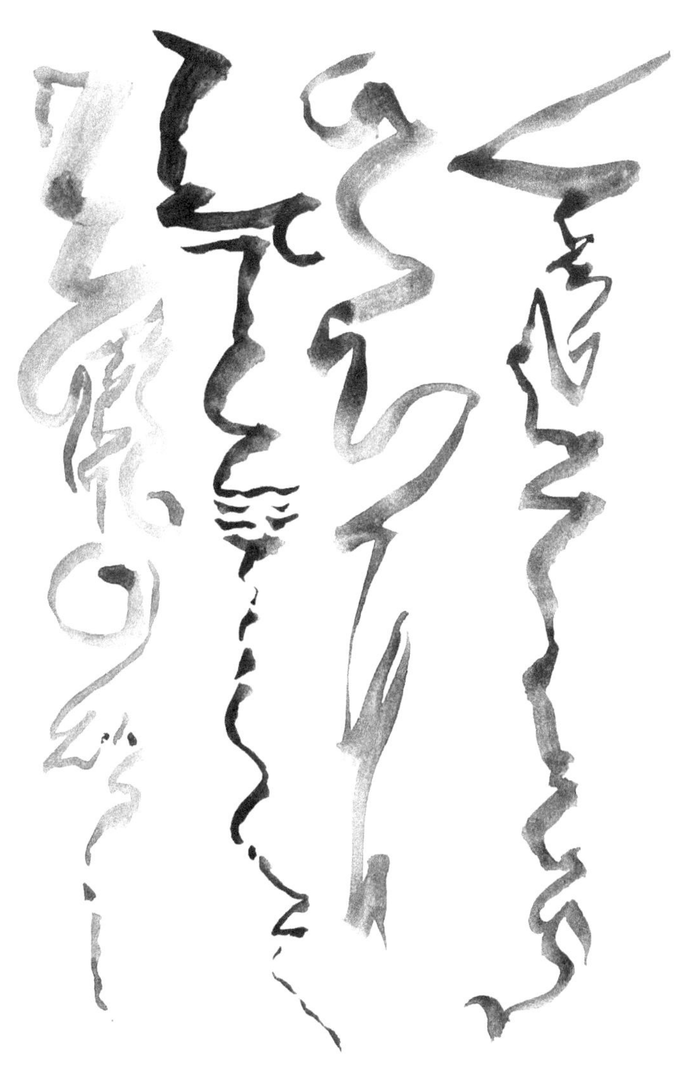

ÉTAIENT

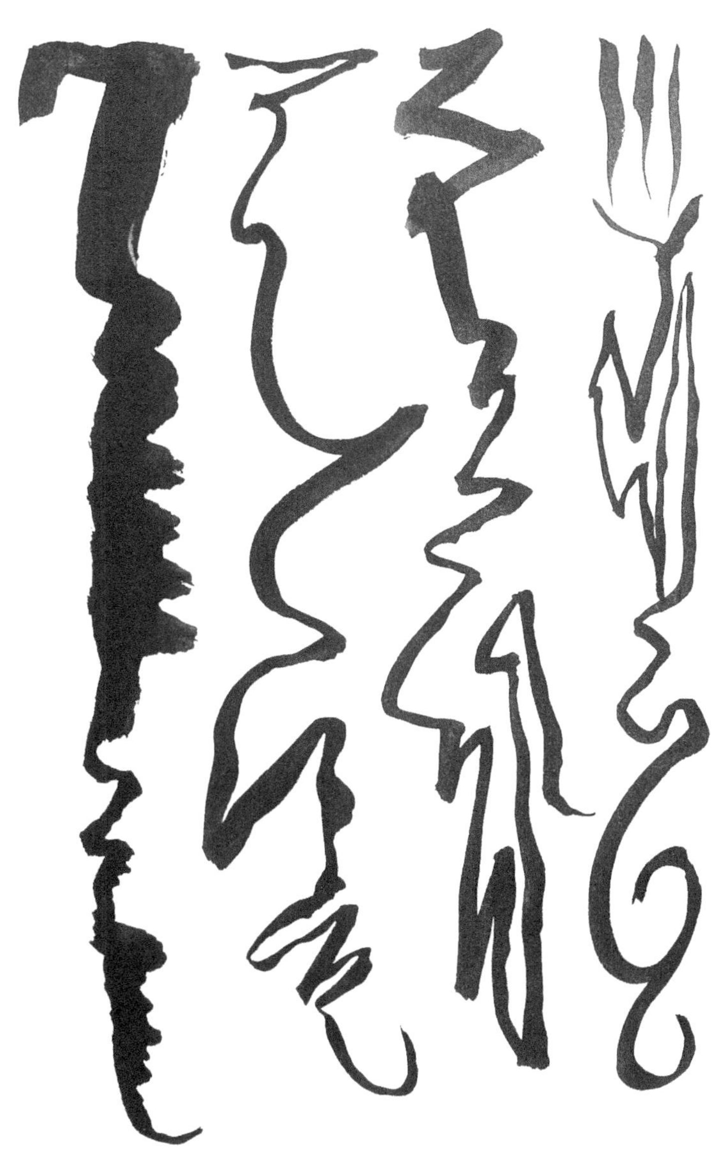

MORTES

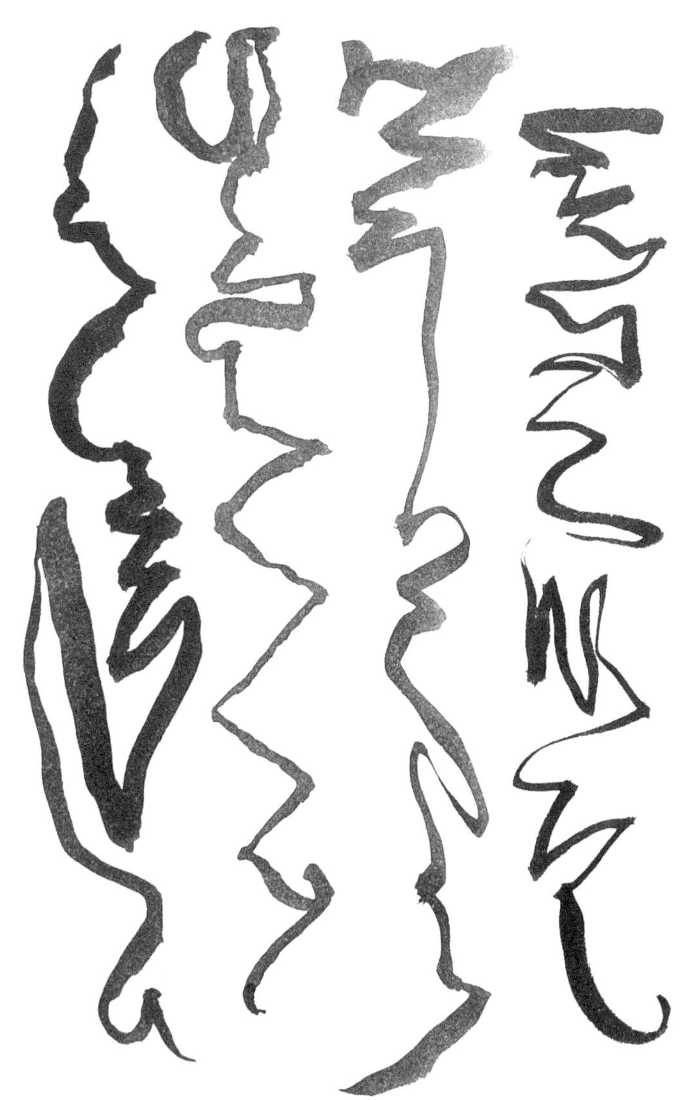

MÊME

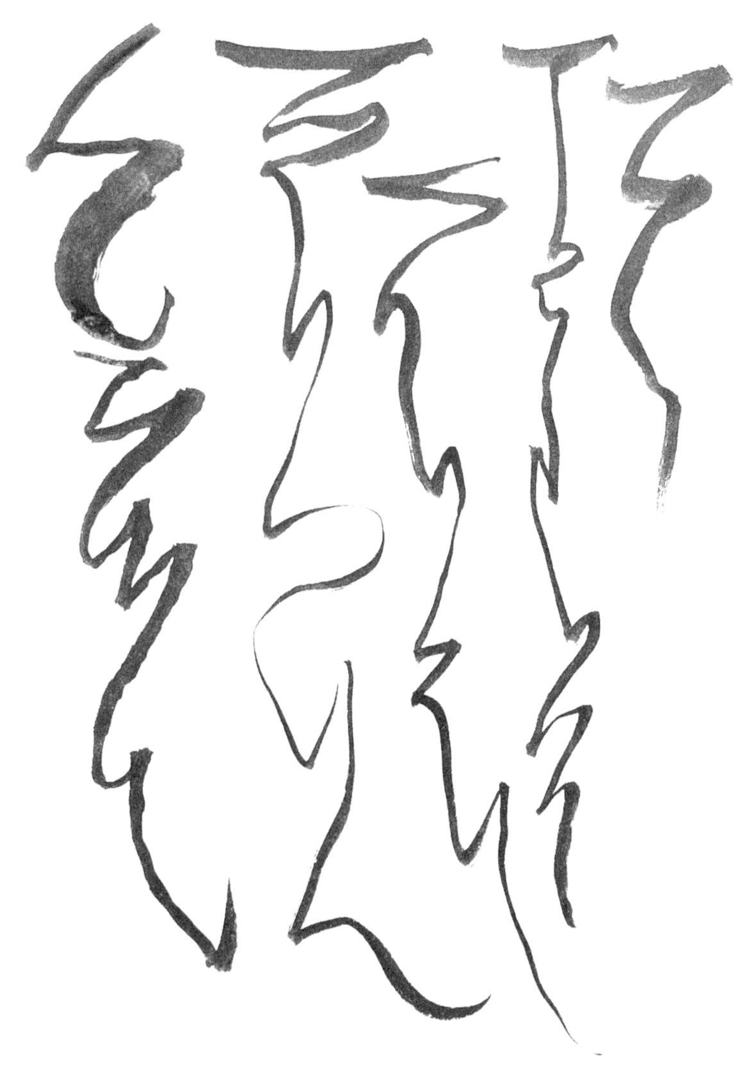

DANS

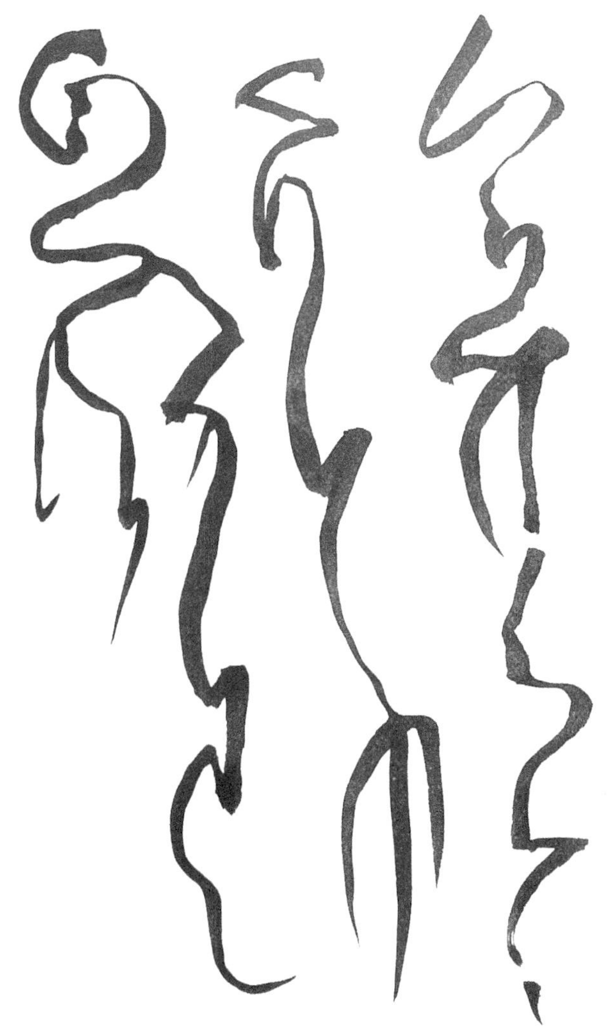

LE

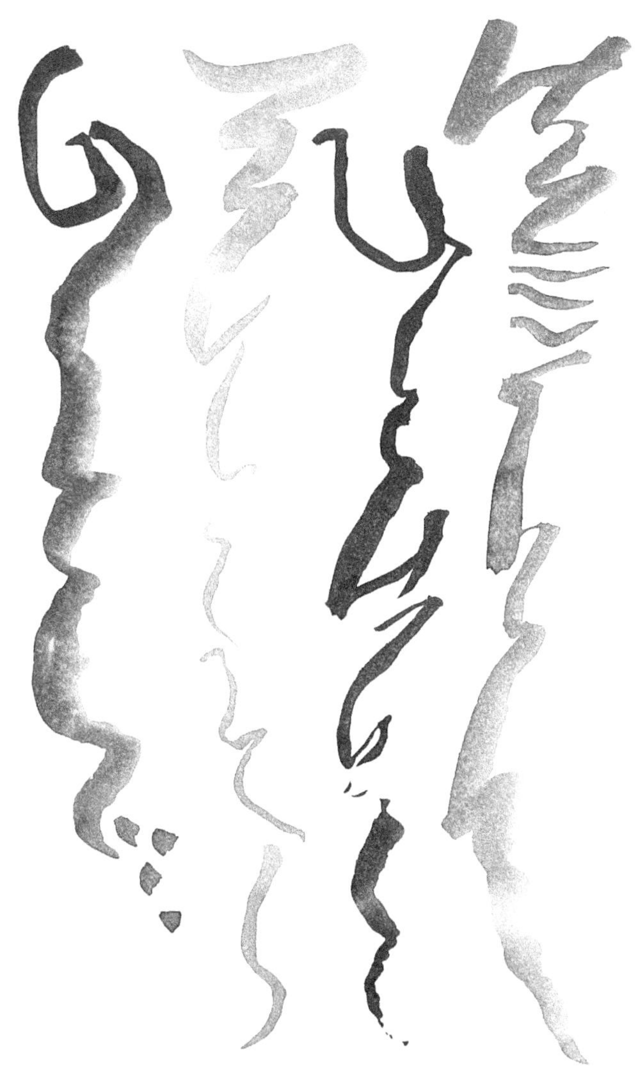

SOUVENIR

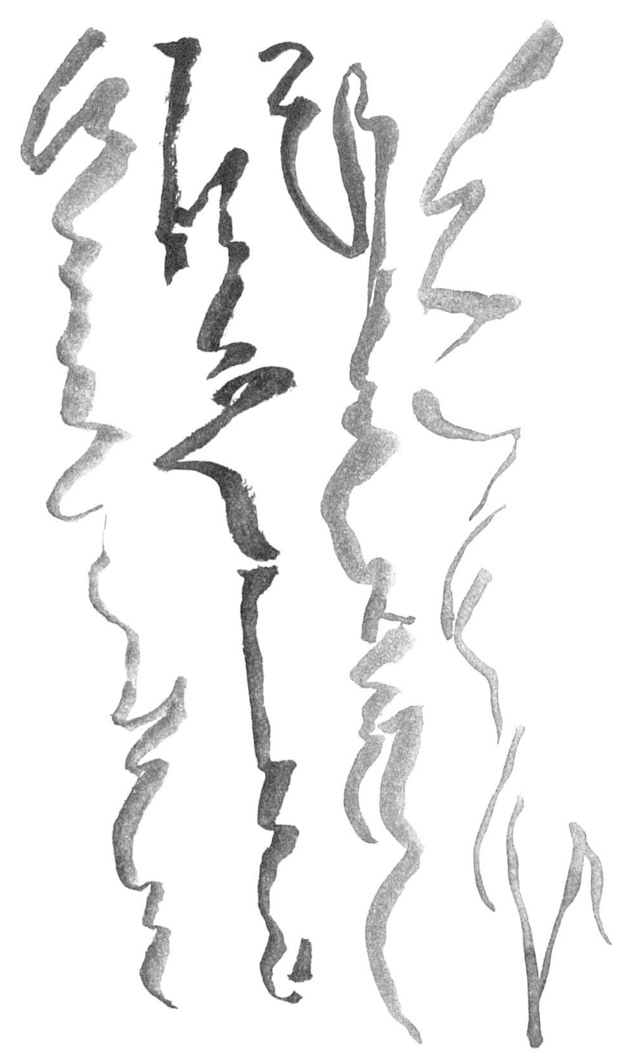

C'EST

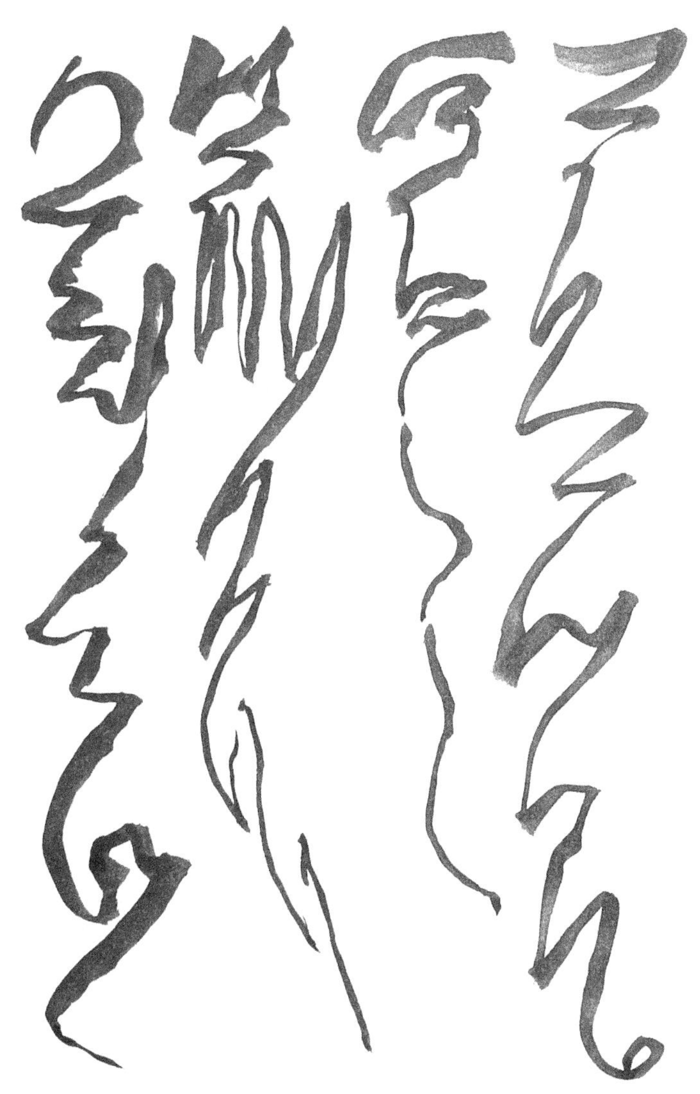

VOUS

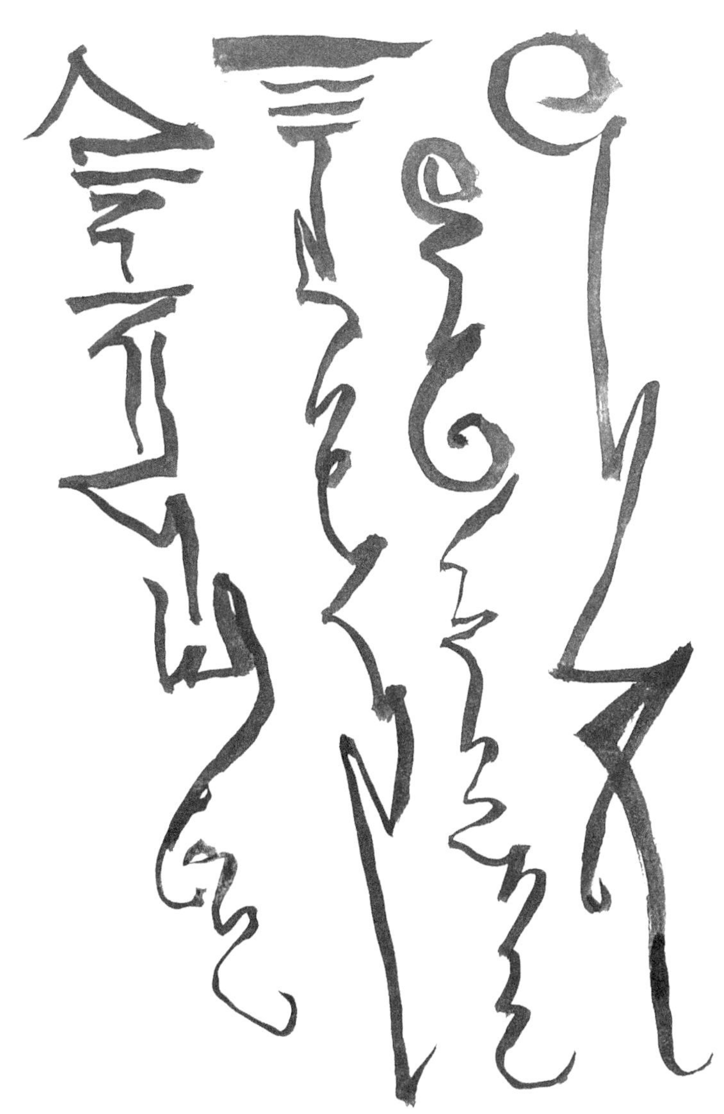

AUSSI

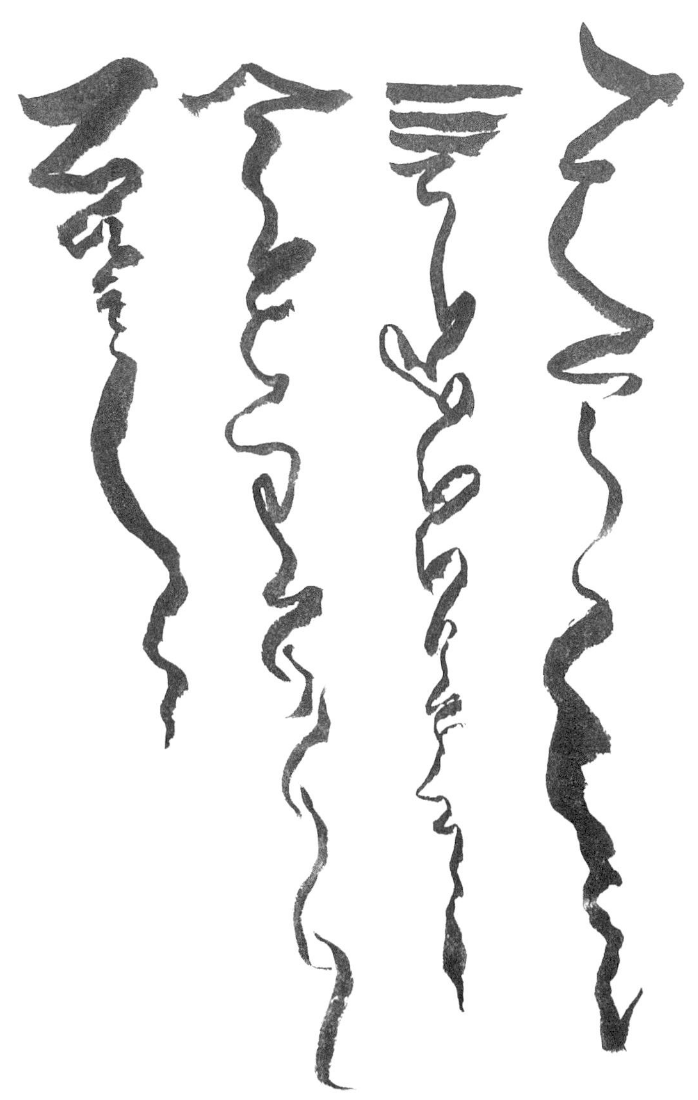

QU'IL

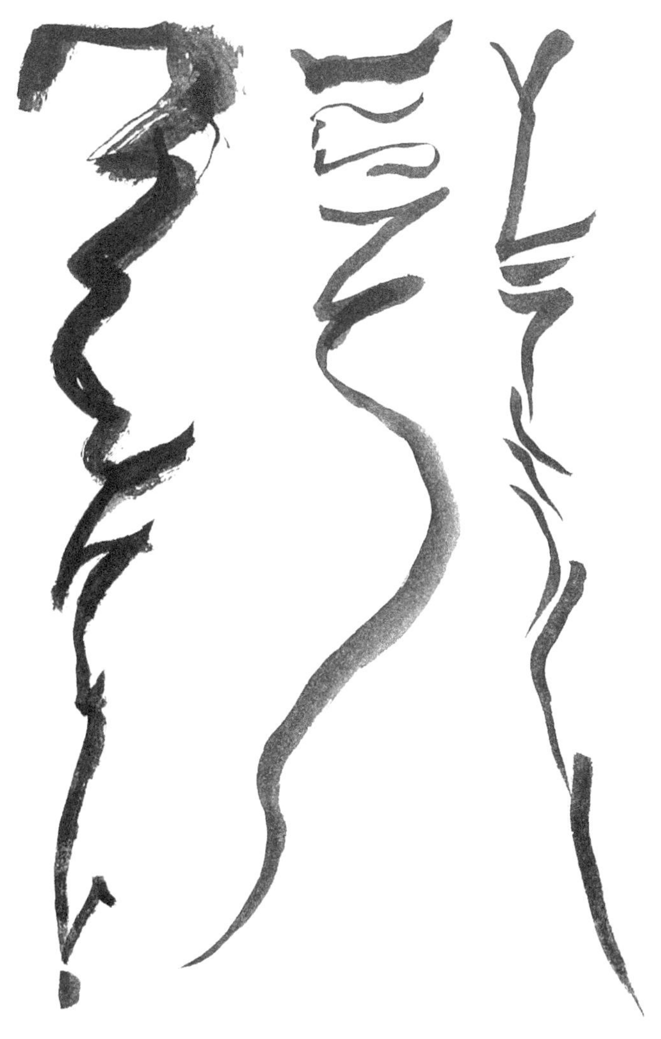

PLEUT

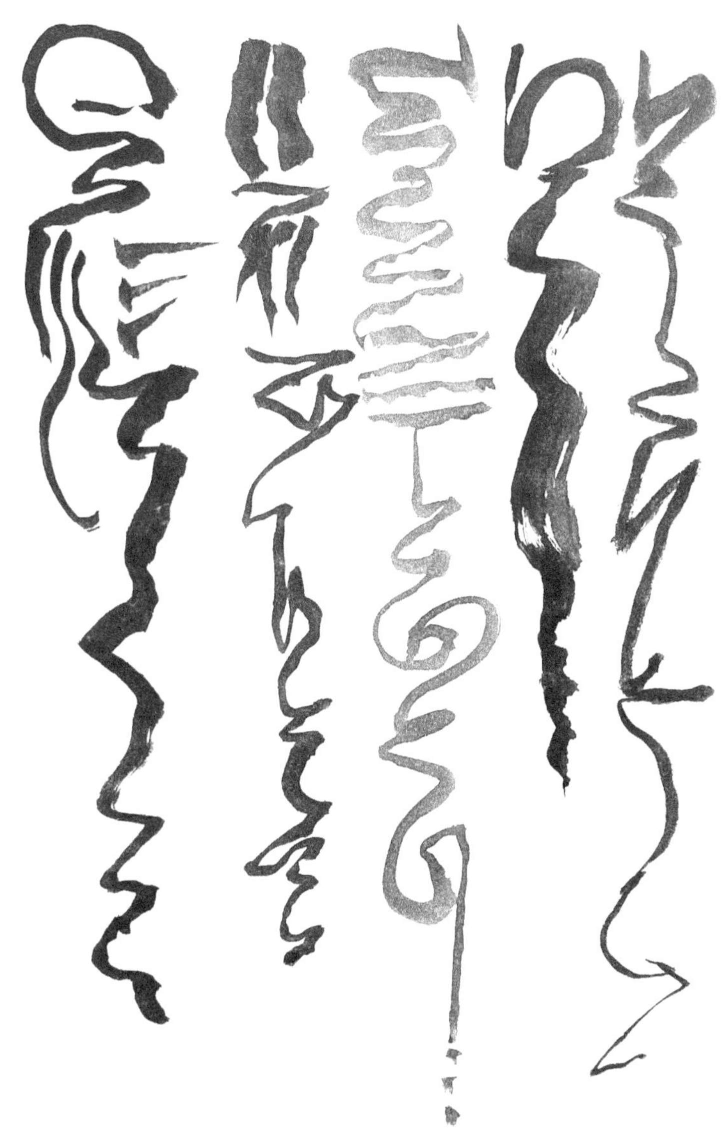

MERVEILLEUSES

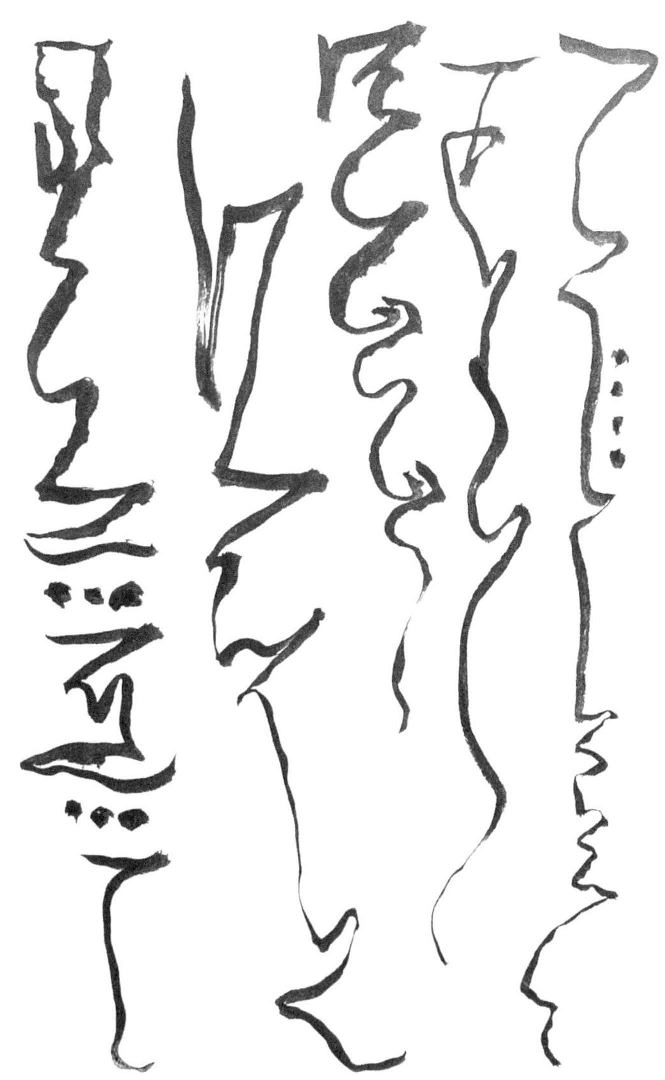

RENCONTRES

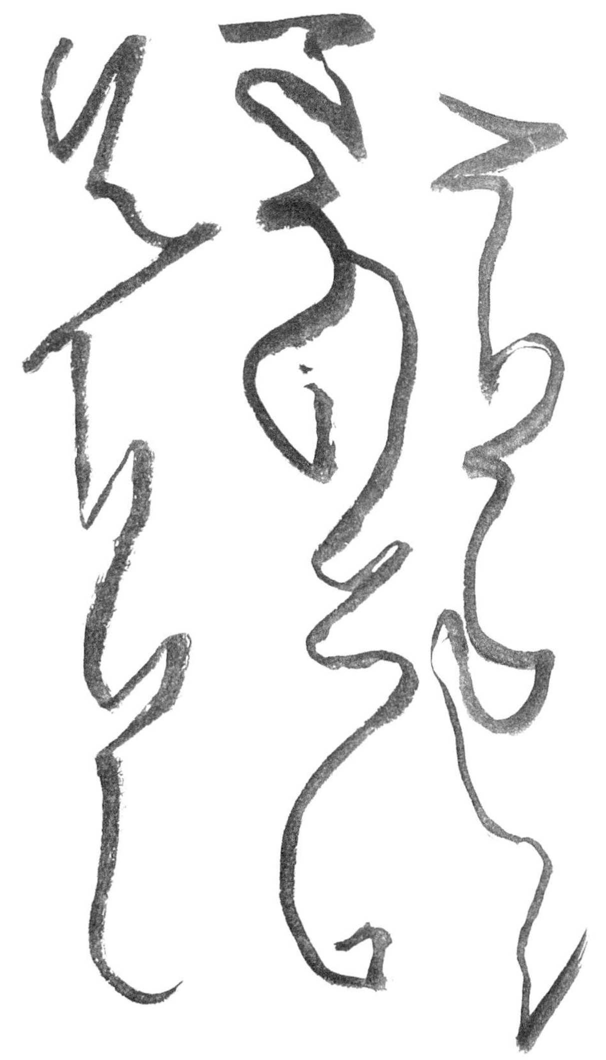

DE

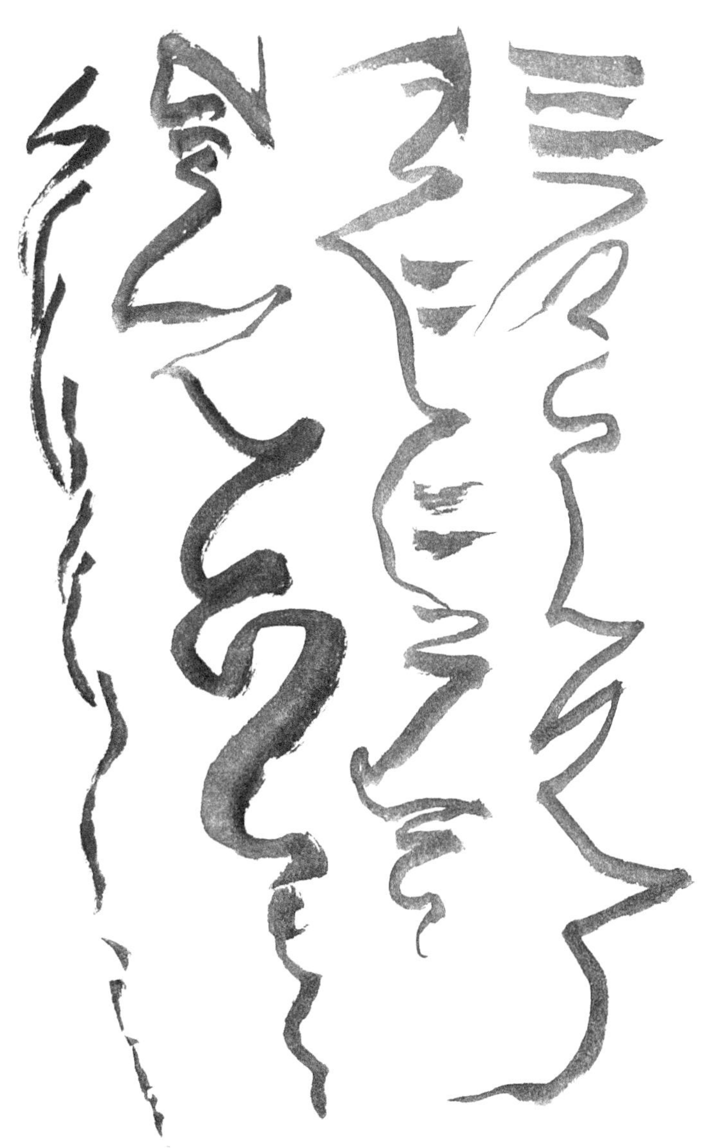

MA

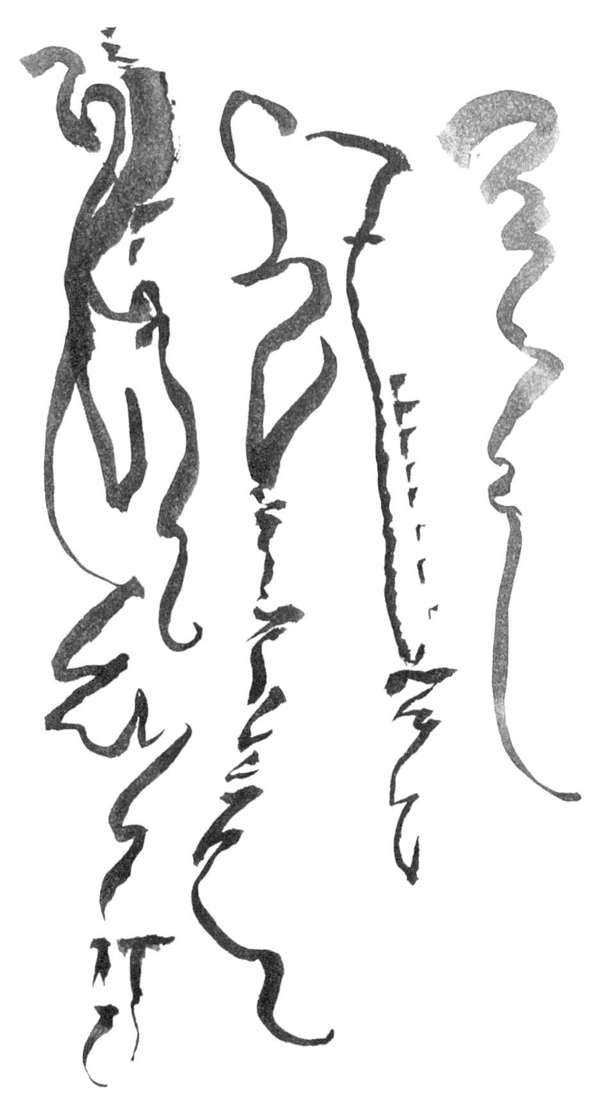

VIE

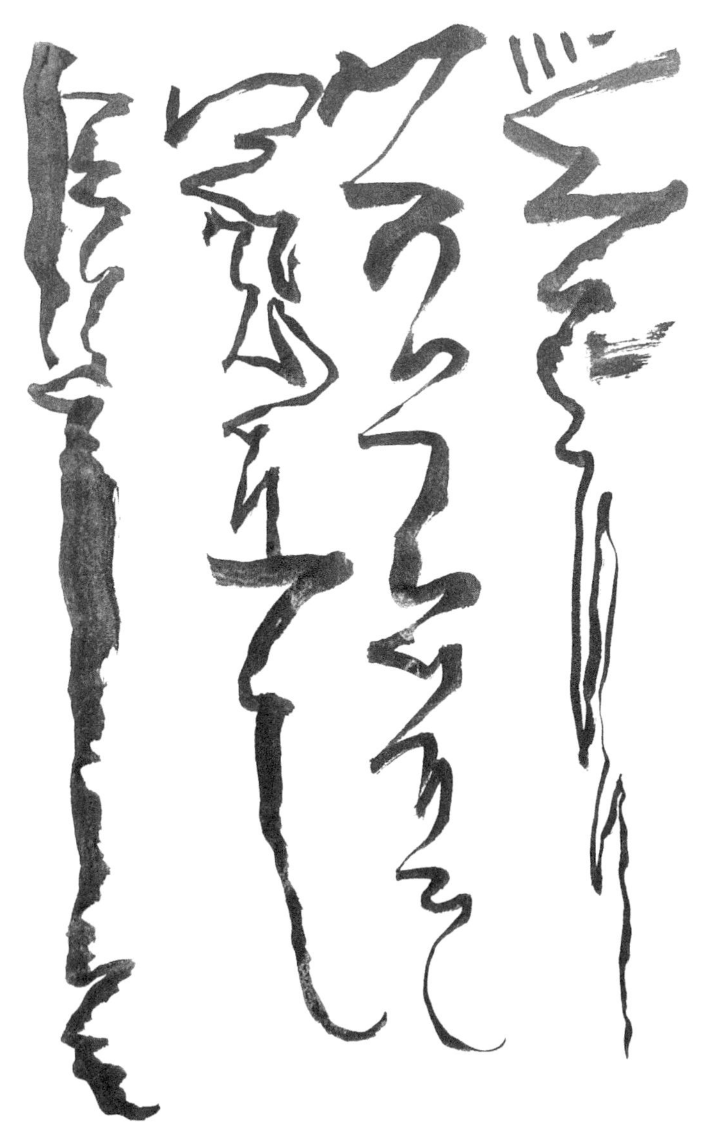

Ô GOUTTELETTES !

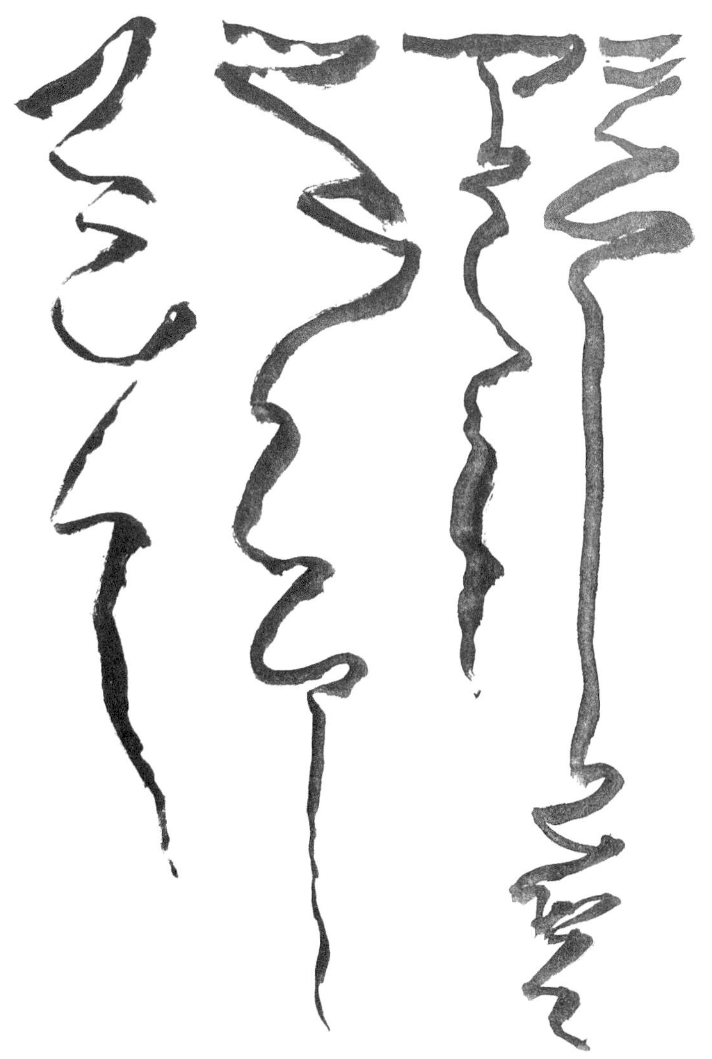

ET

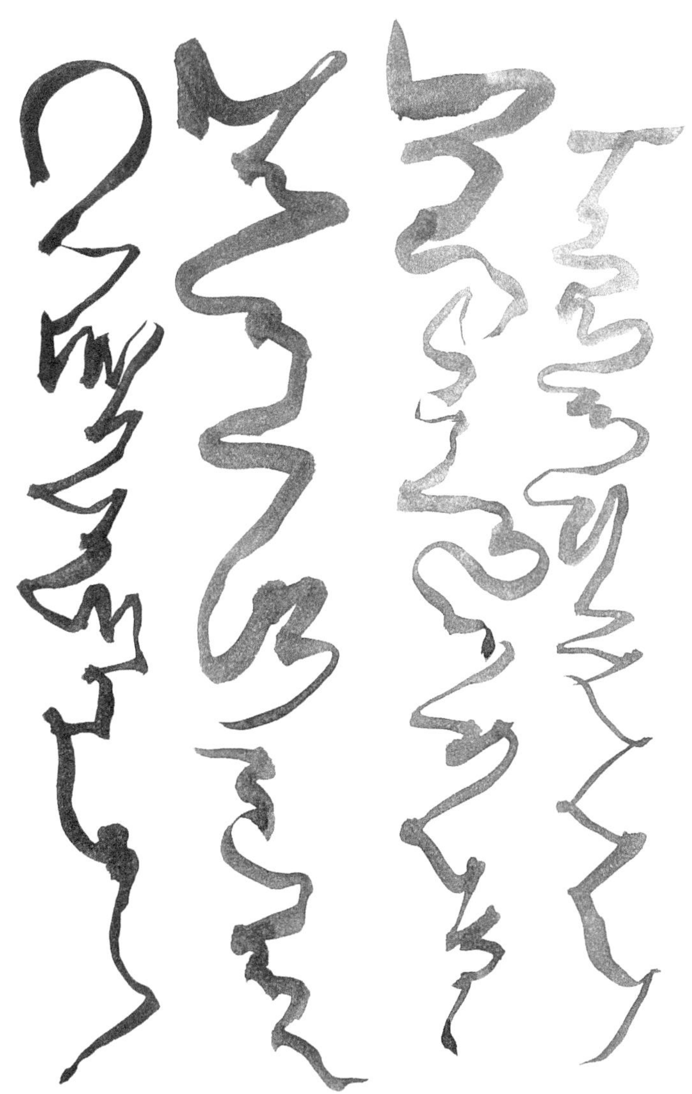

CES

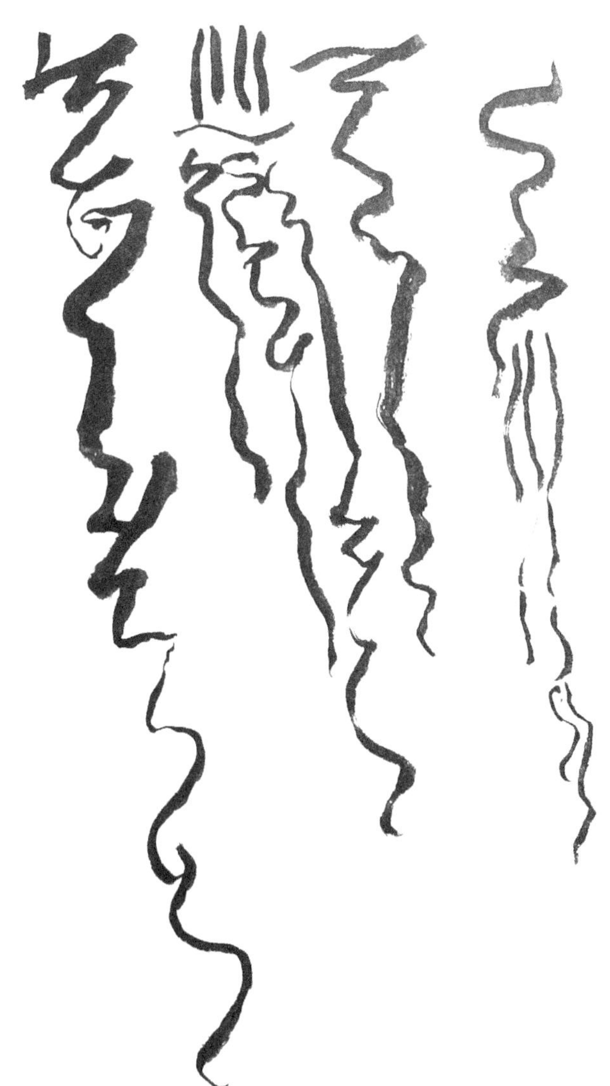

NUAGES

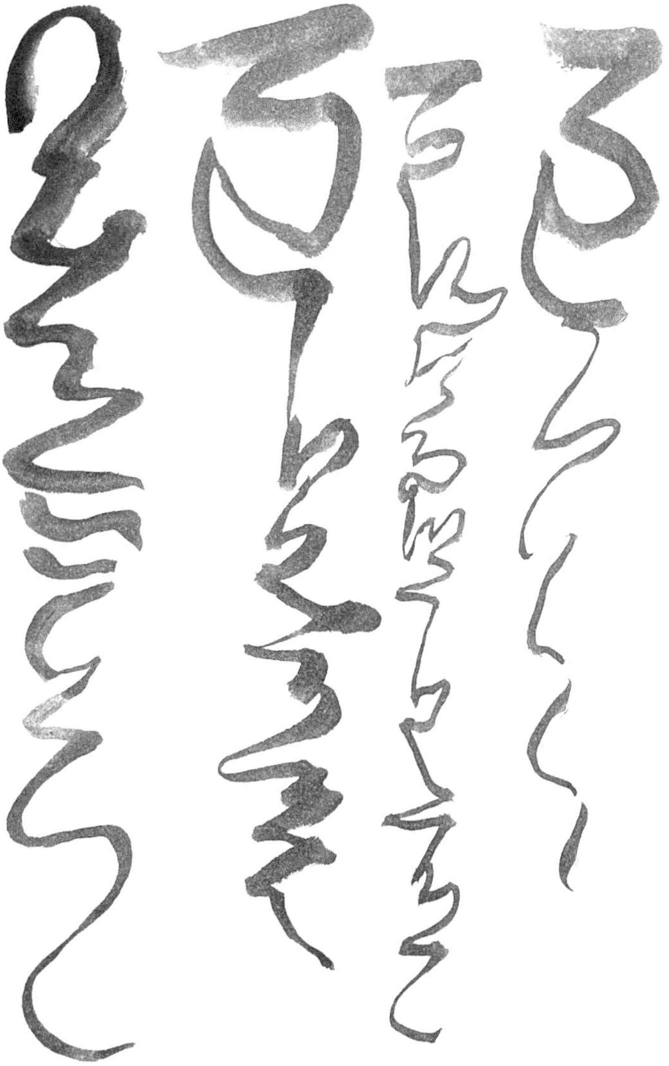

CABRÉS

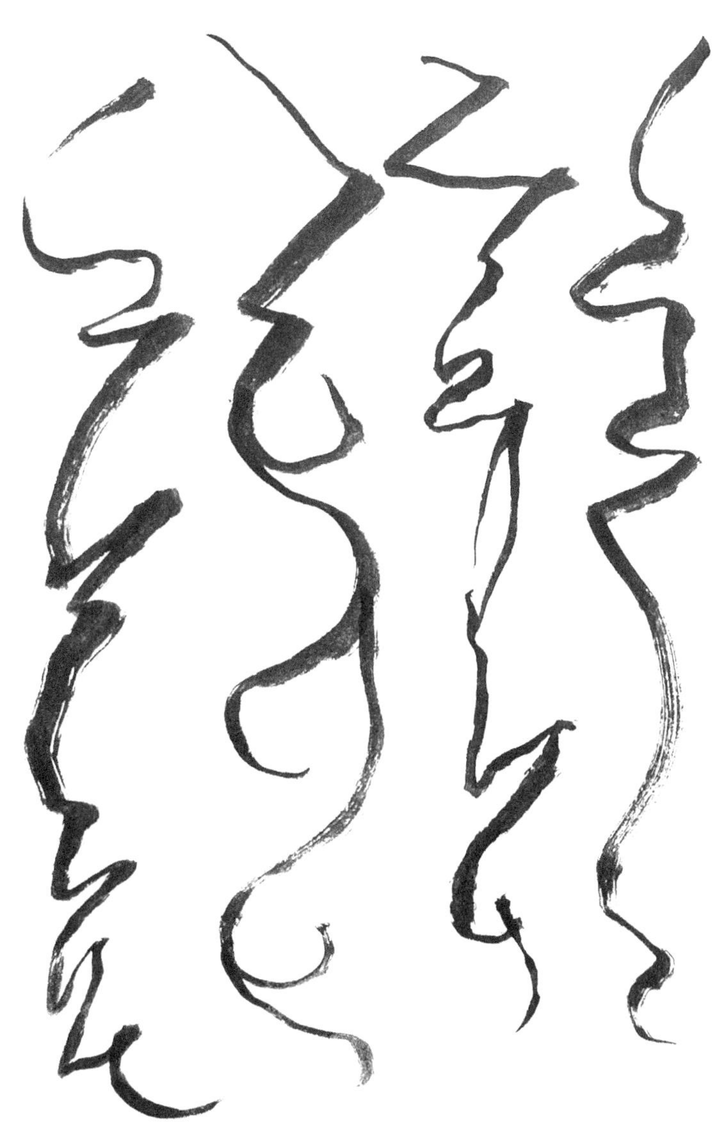

SE

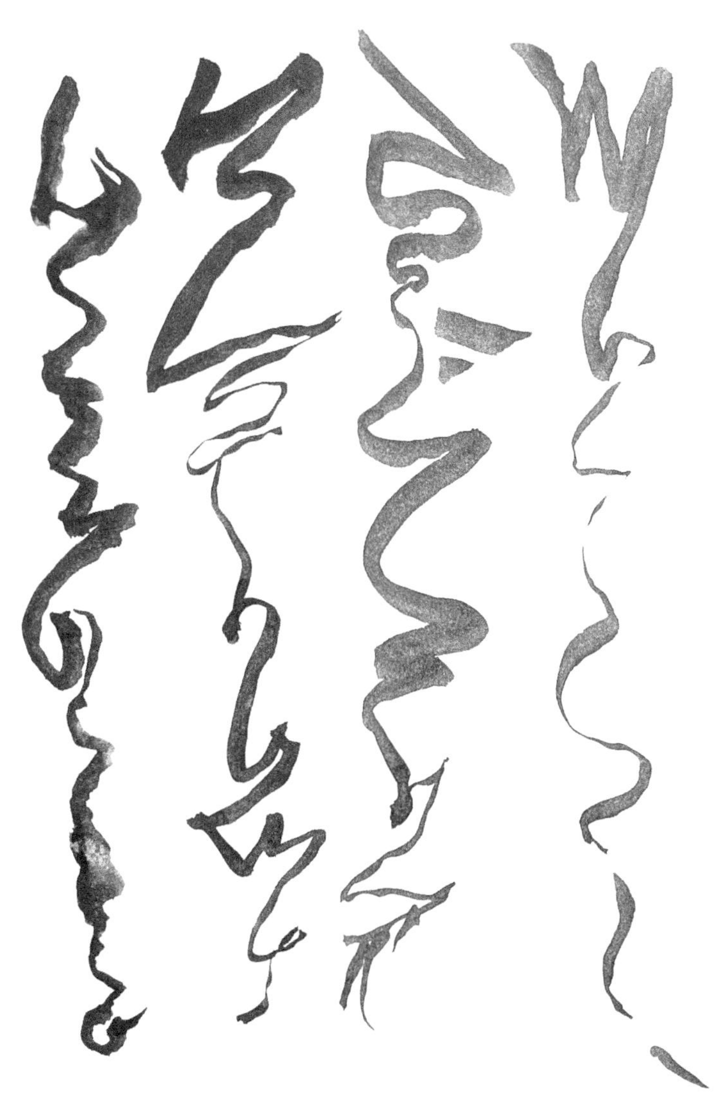

PRENNENT

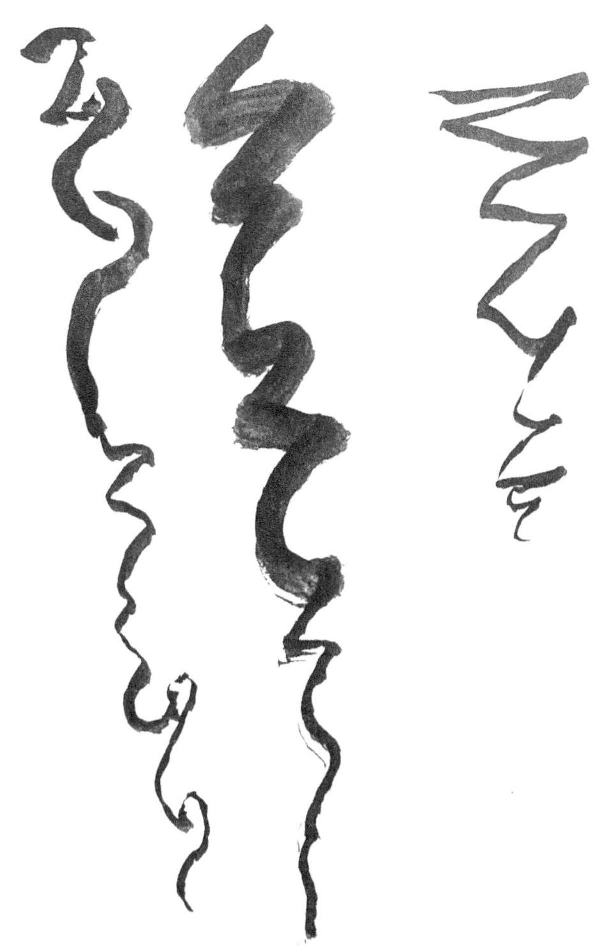

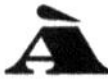

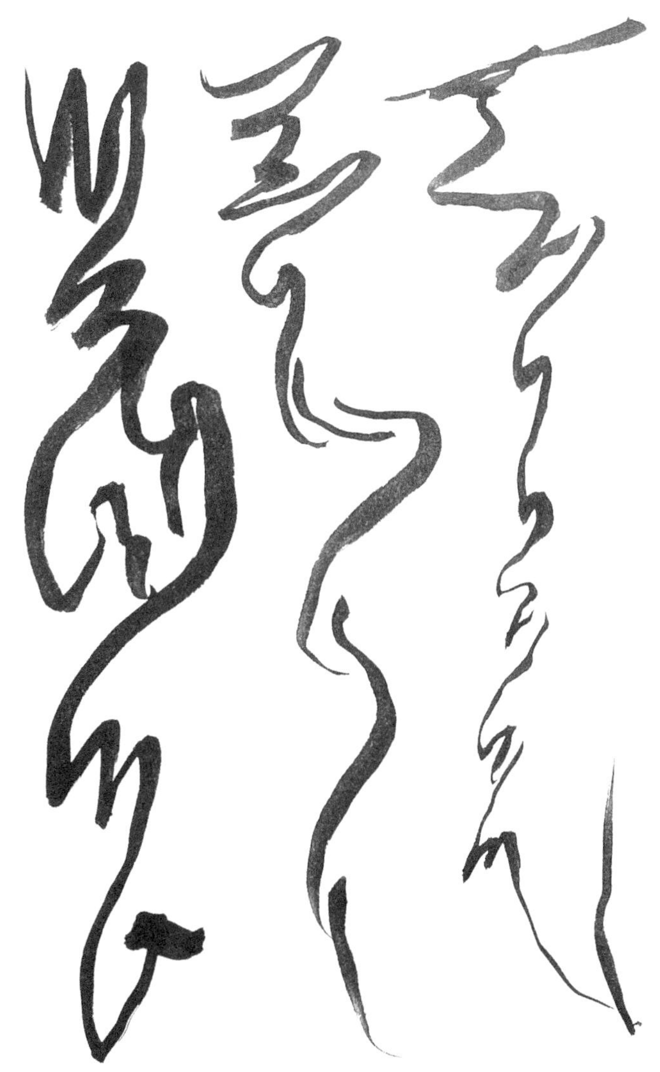

HENNIR

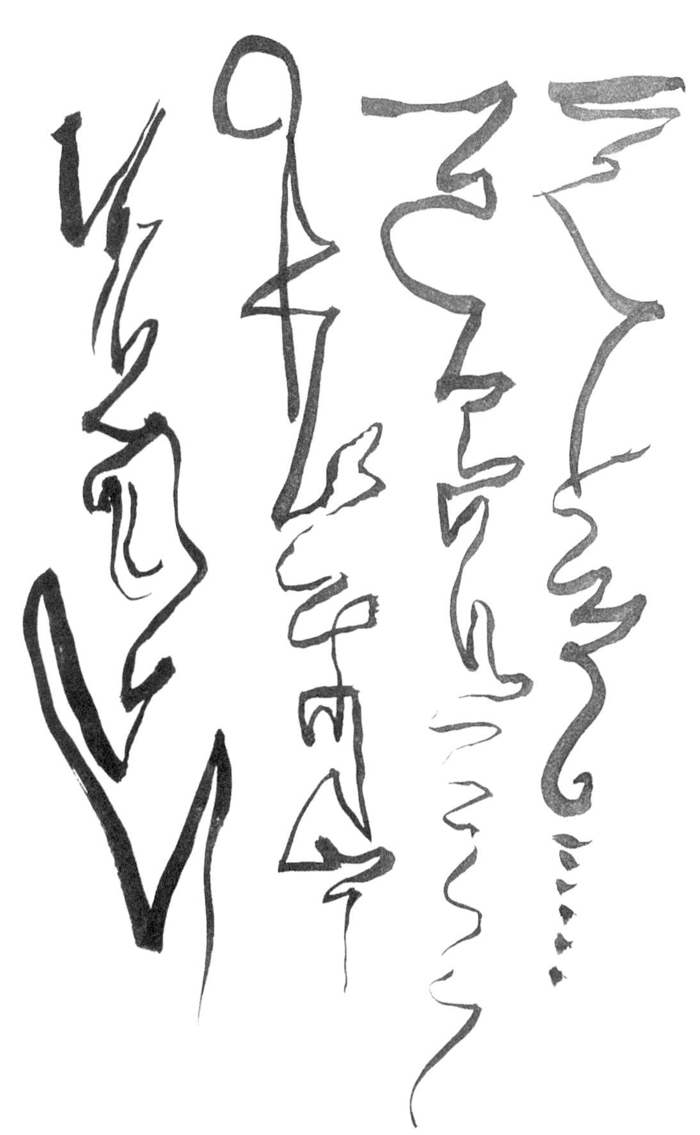

TOUT

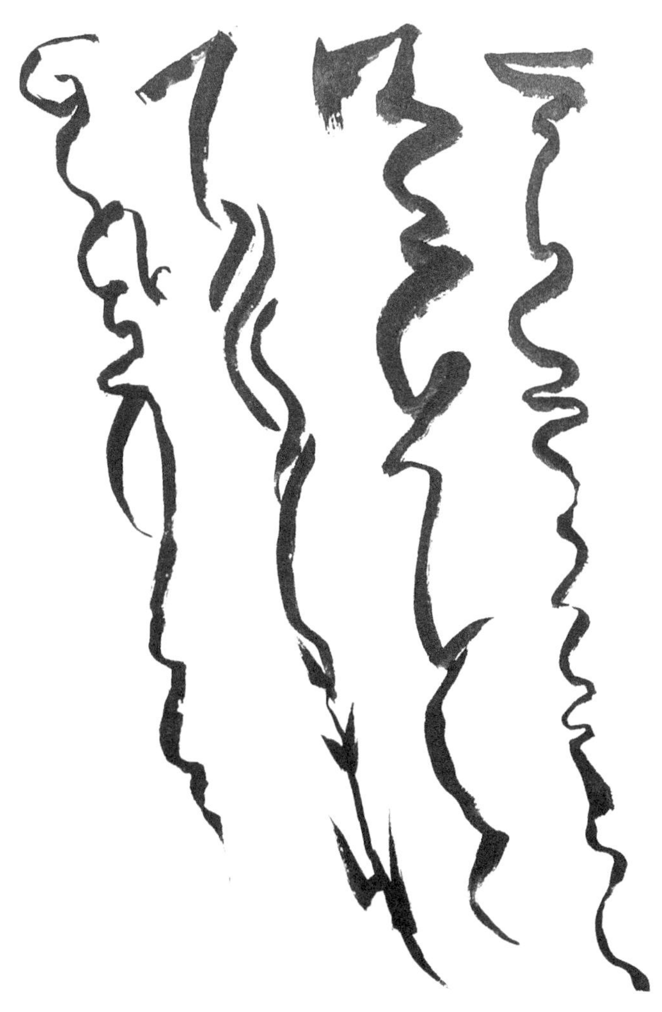

UN

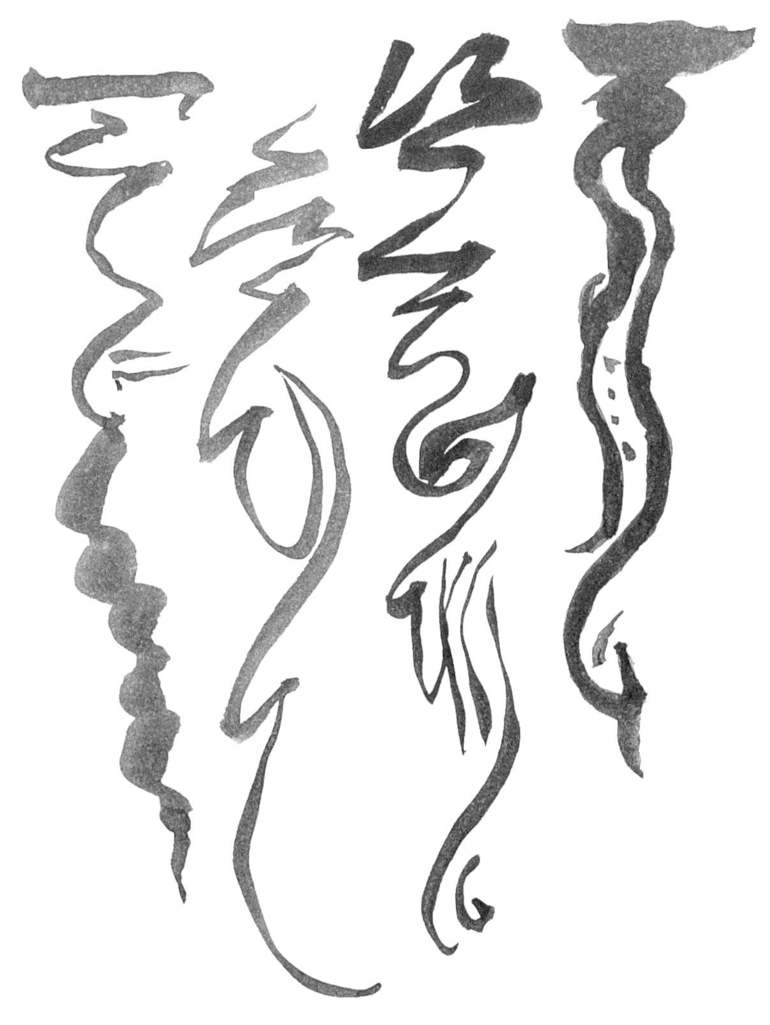

UNIVERS

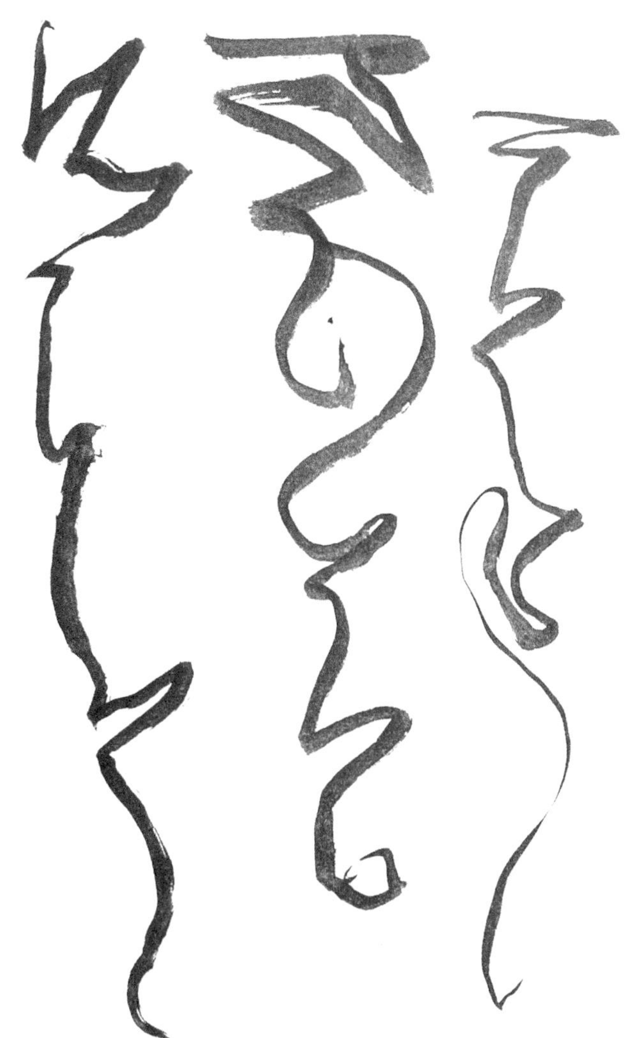

DE

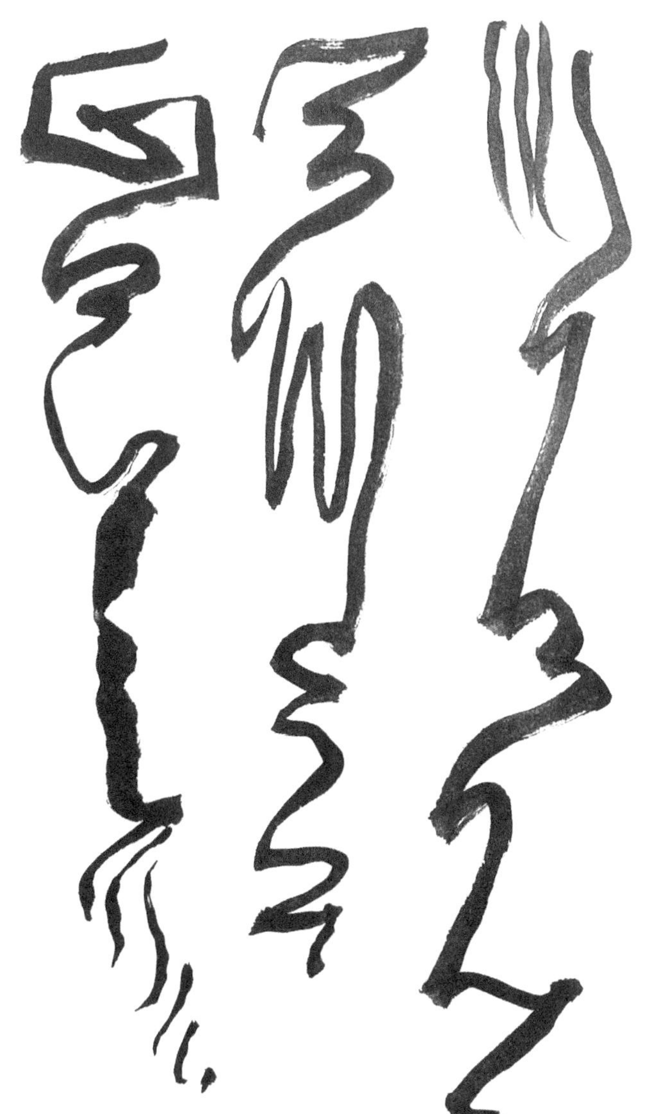

VILLES

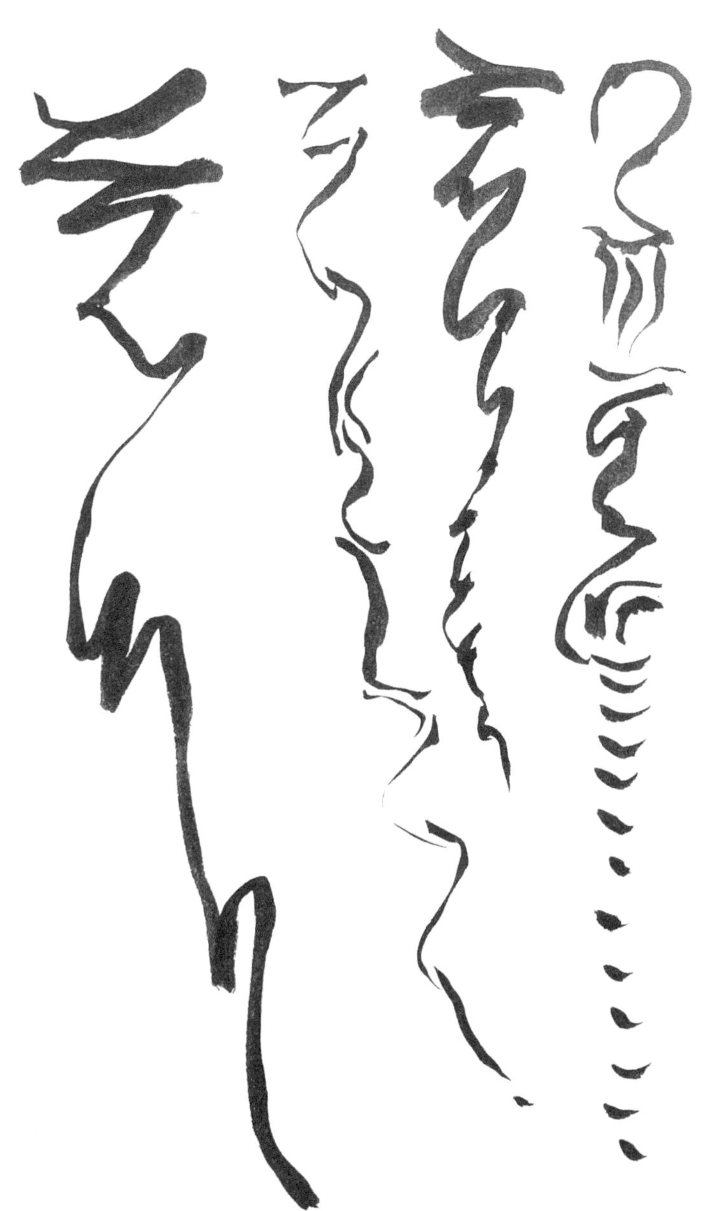

AURICULAIRES

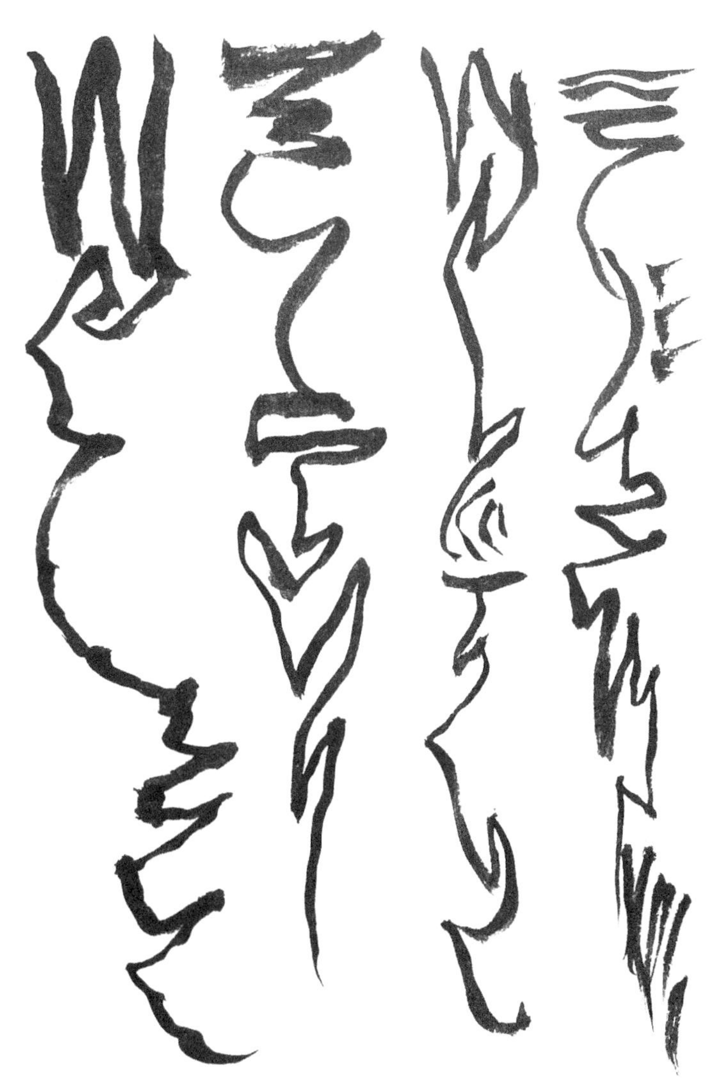

ÉCOUT

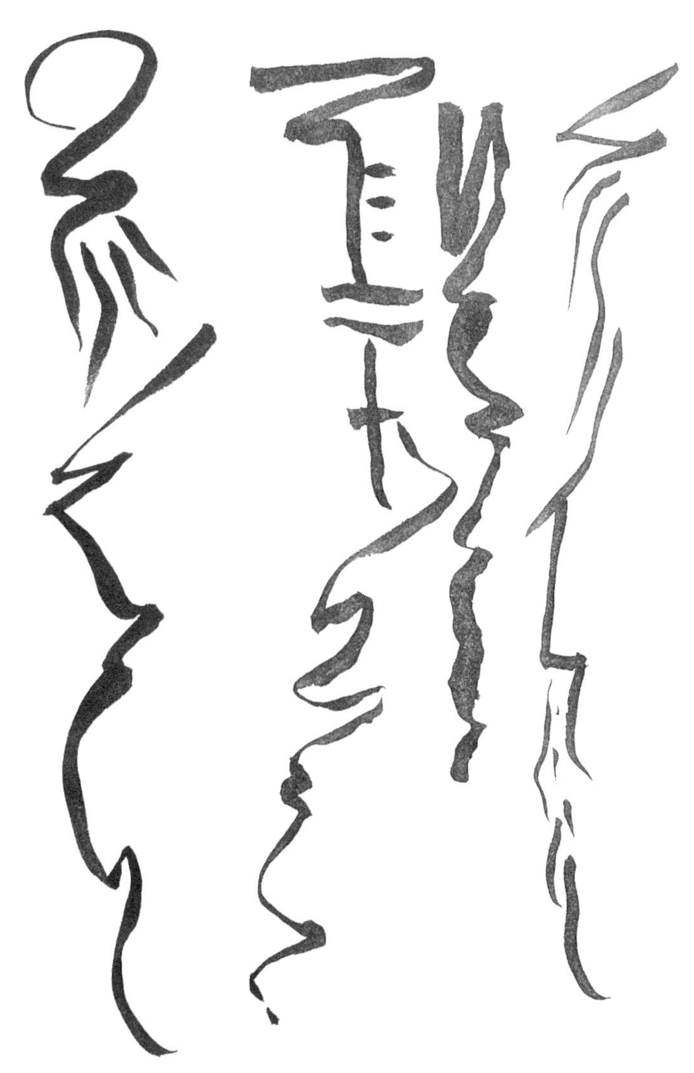

S'IL

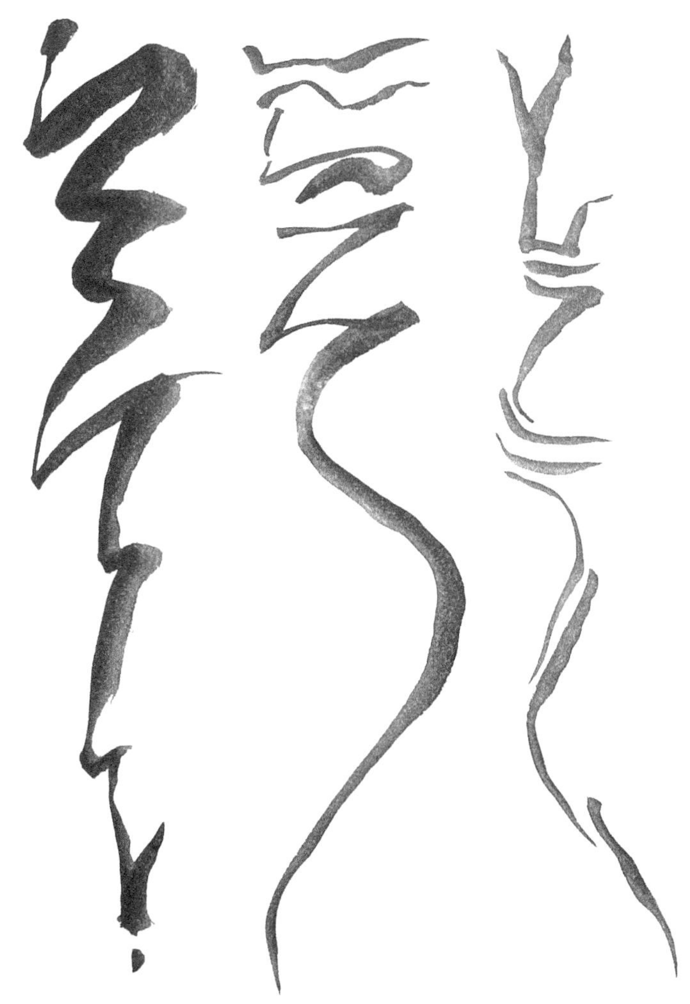

PLEUT

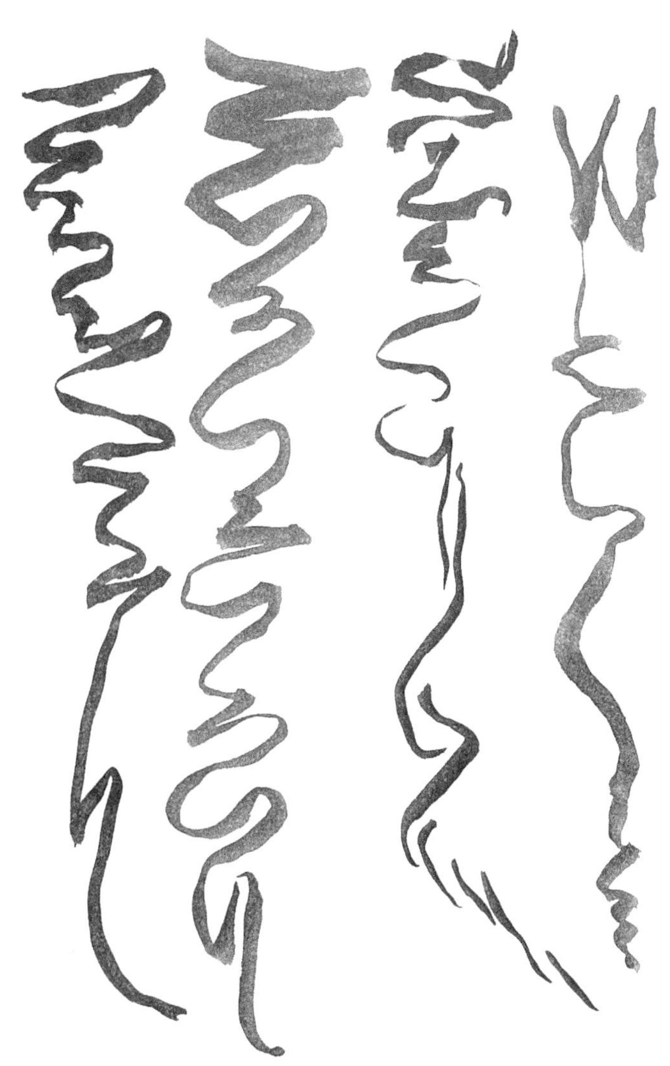

TANDIS

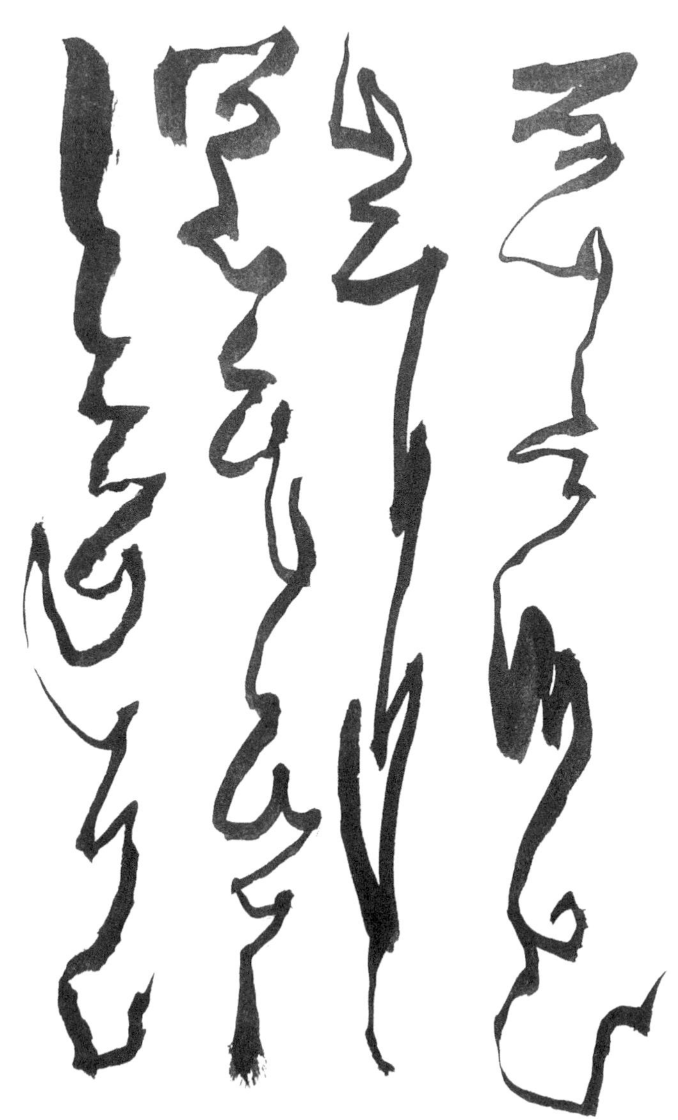

QUE

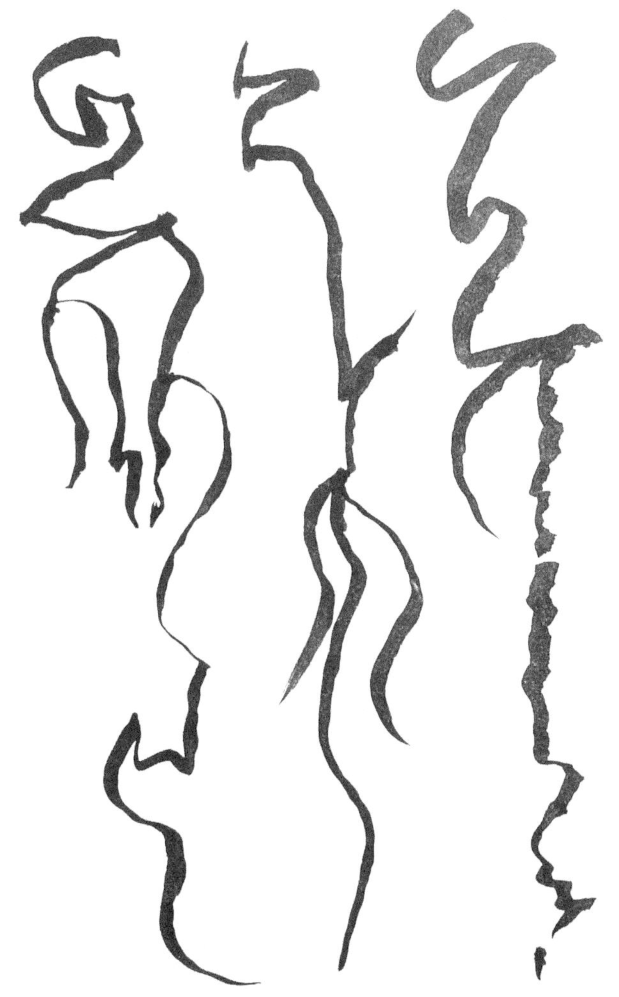

LE

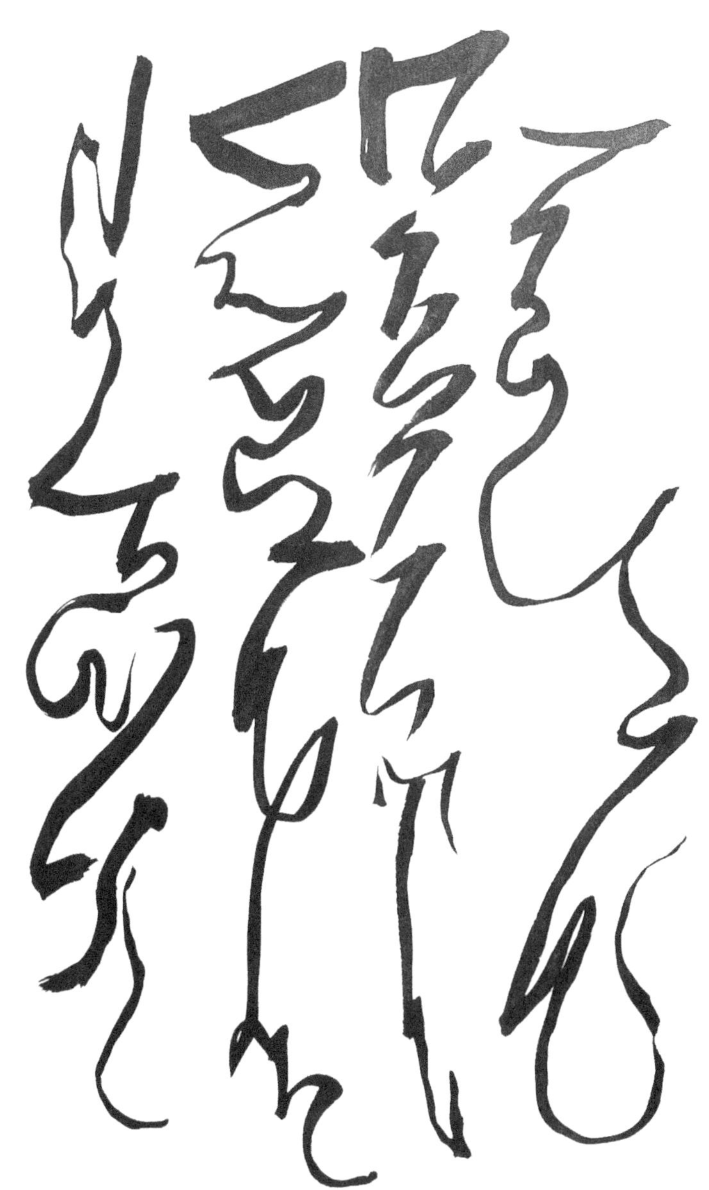

REGRET

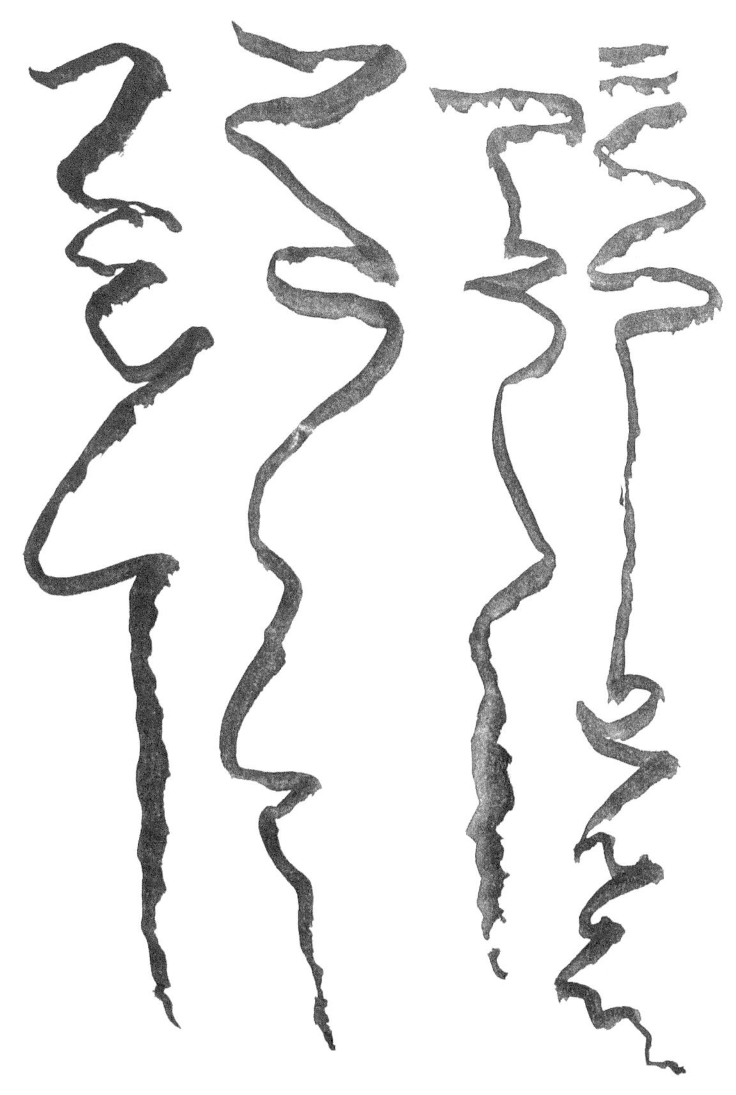

ET

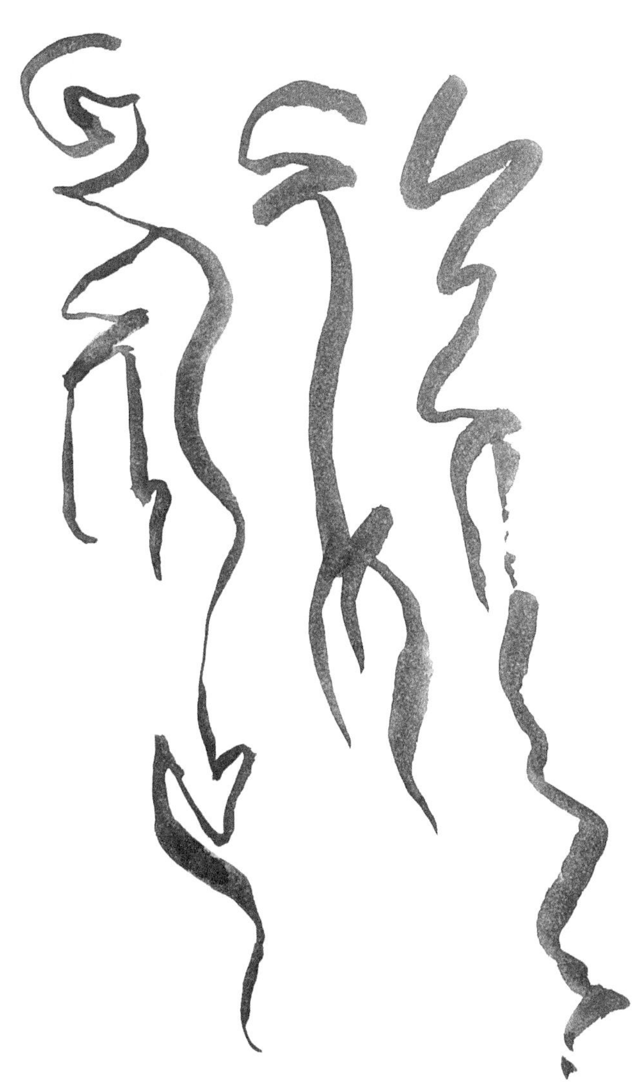

LE

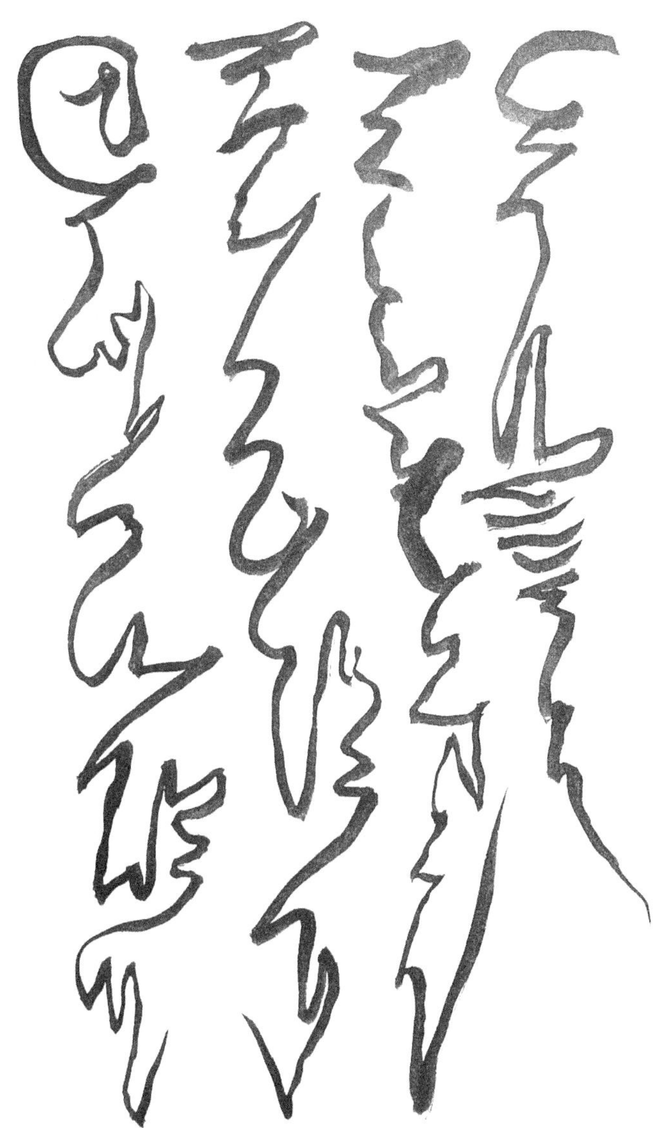

DÉDAIN

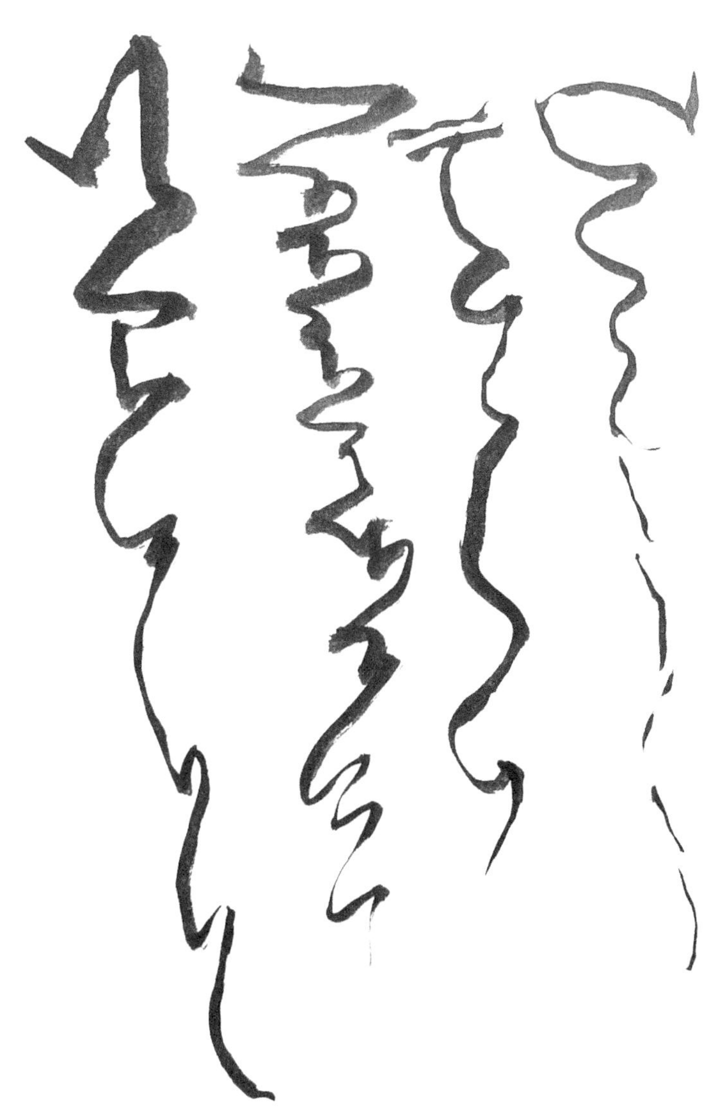

PLEURENT

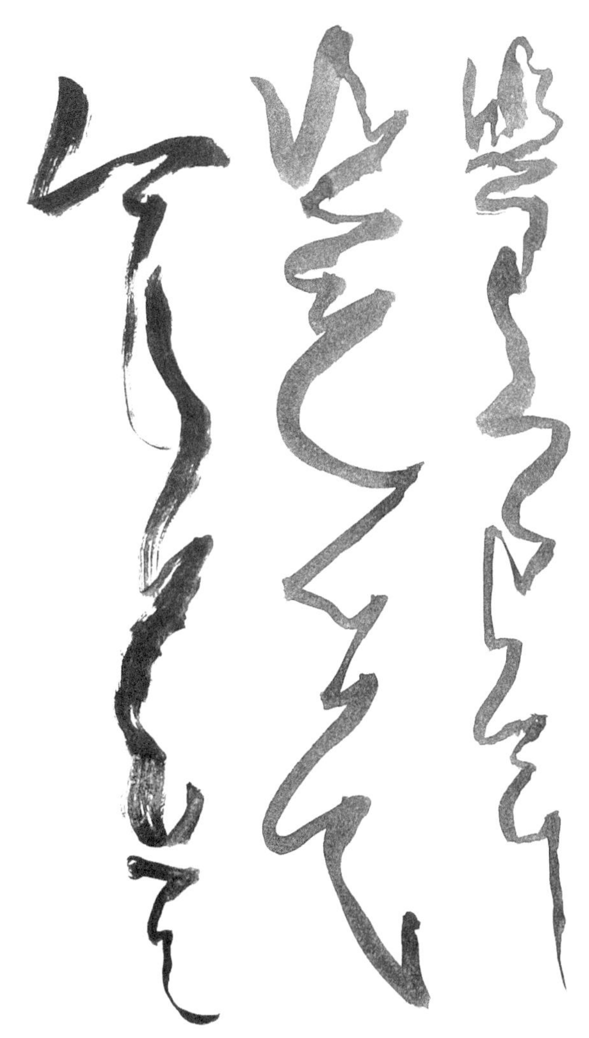

UNE

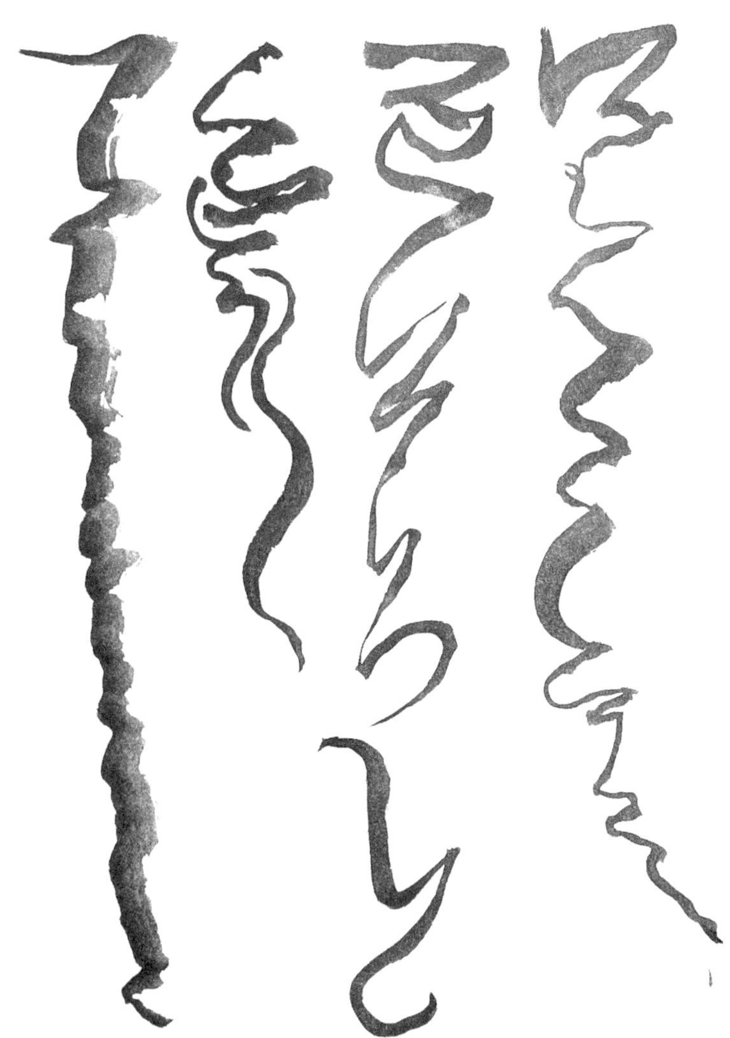

ANCIENNE

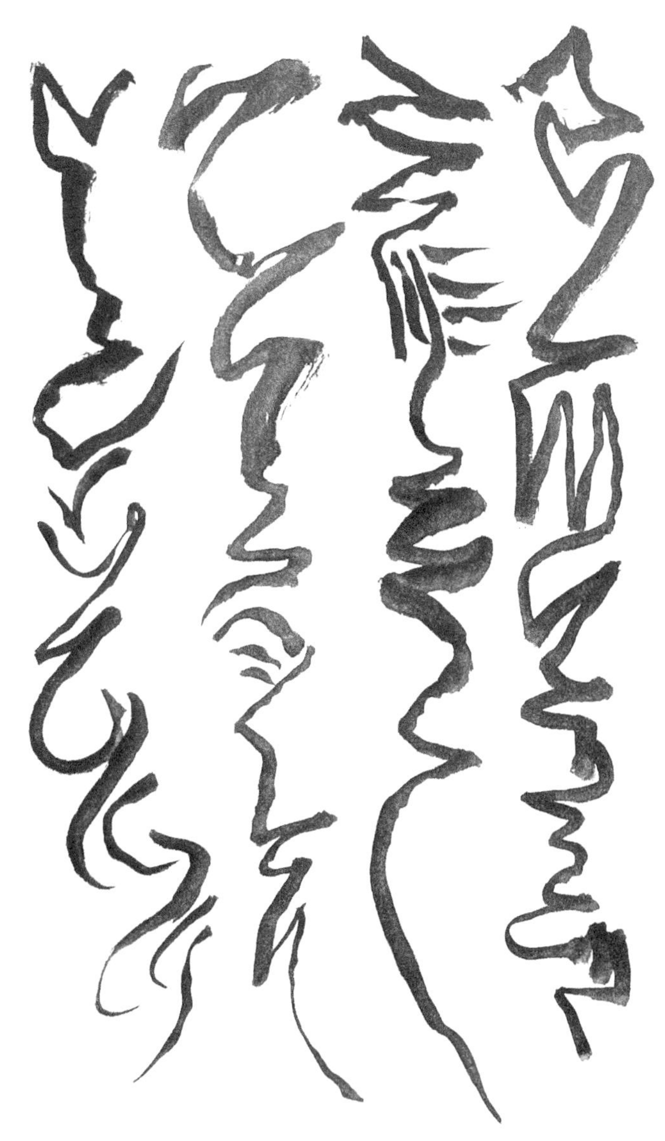

MUSIQUE

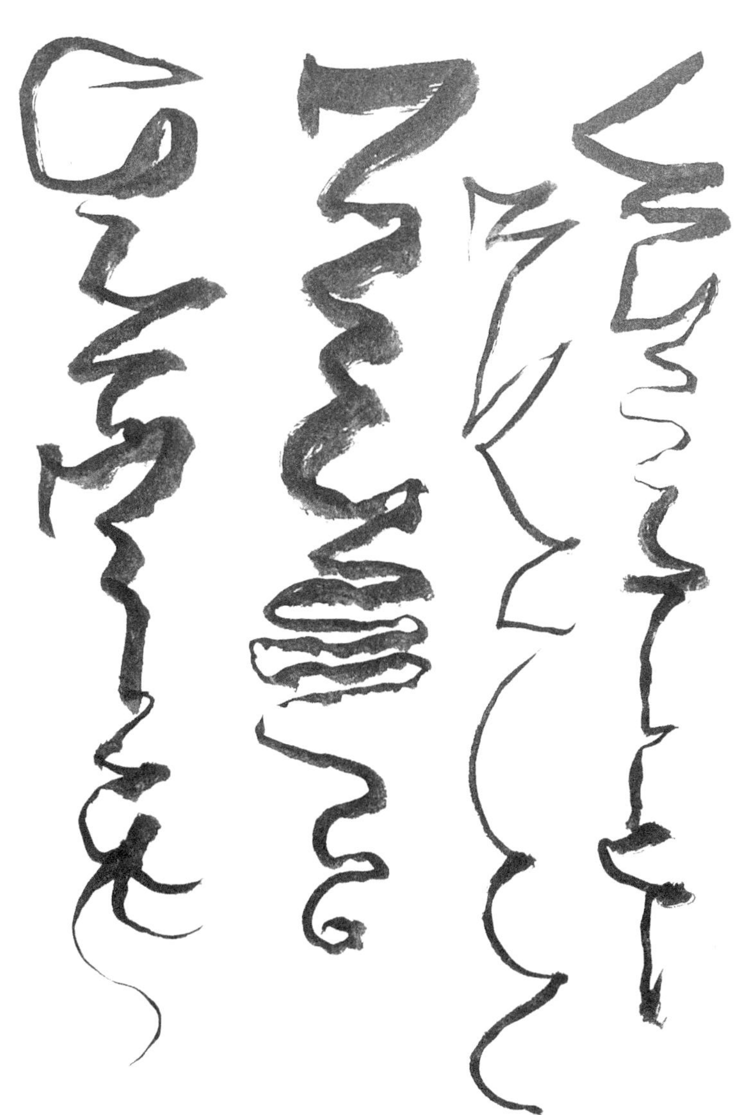

ÉCOUTE

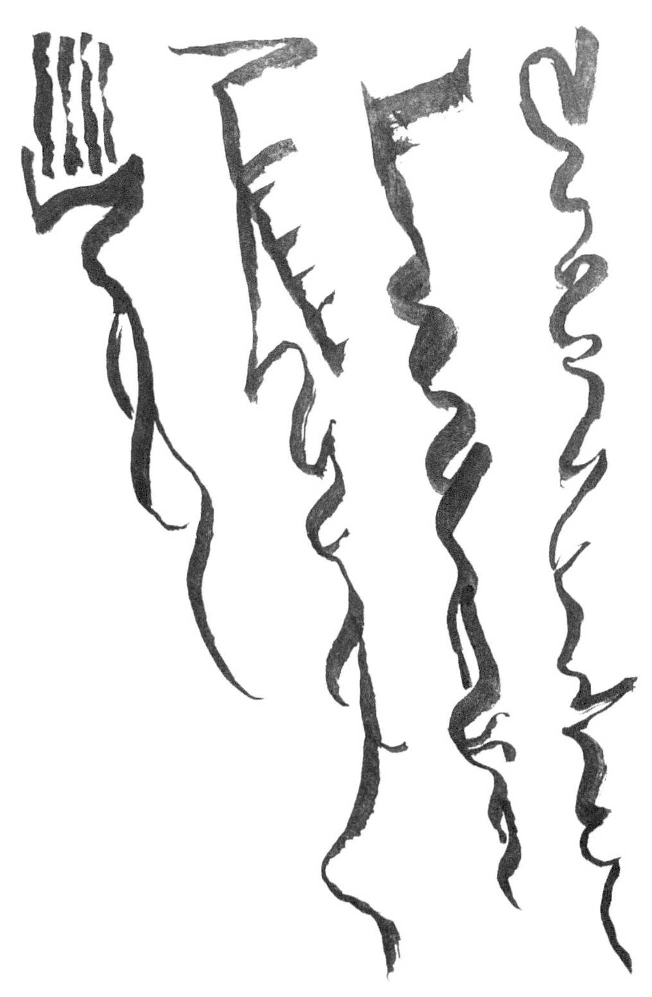

TOMBER

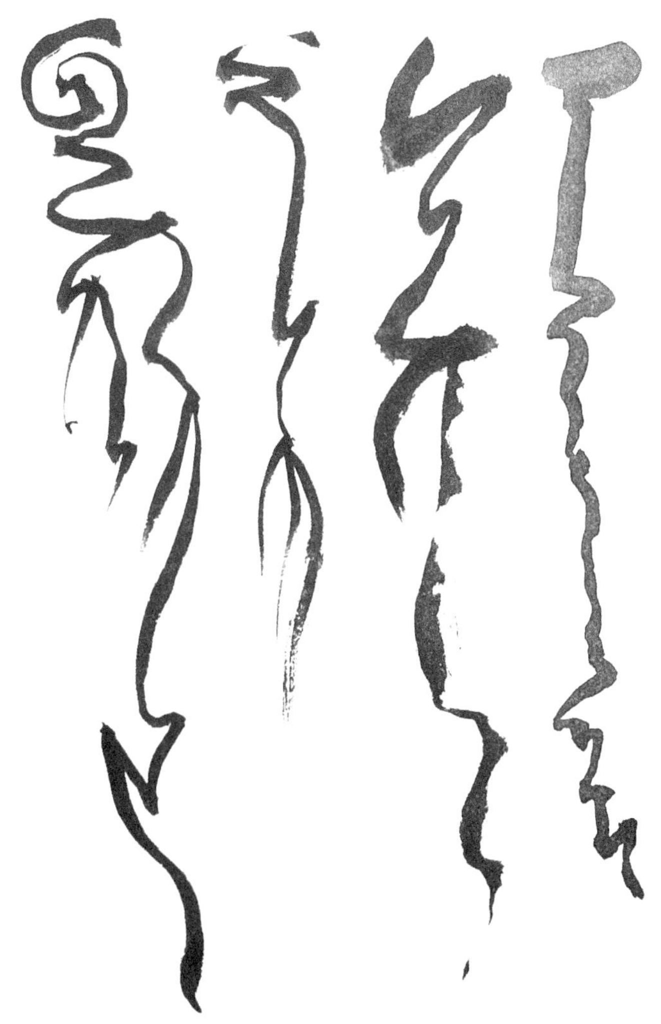

LES

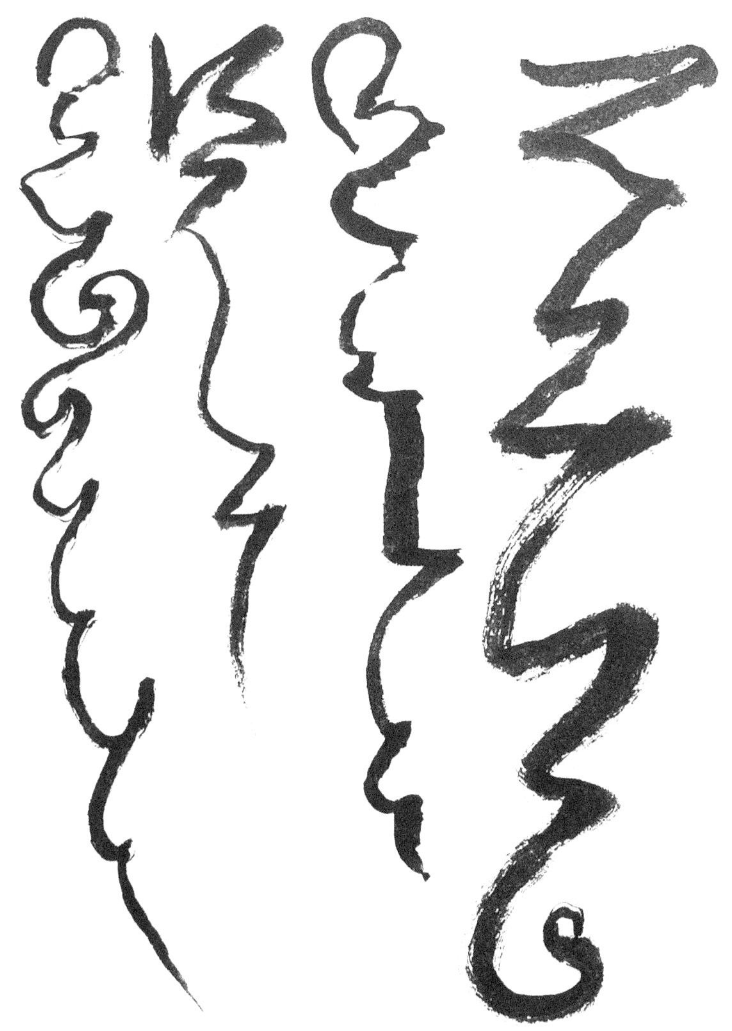

LIENS

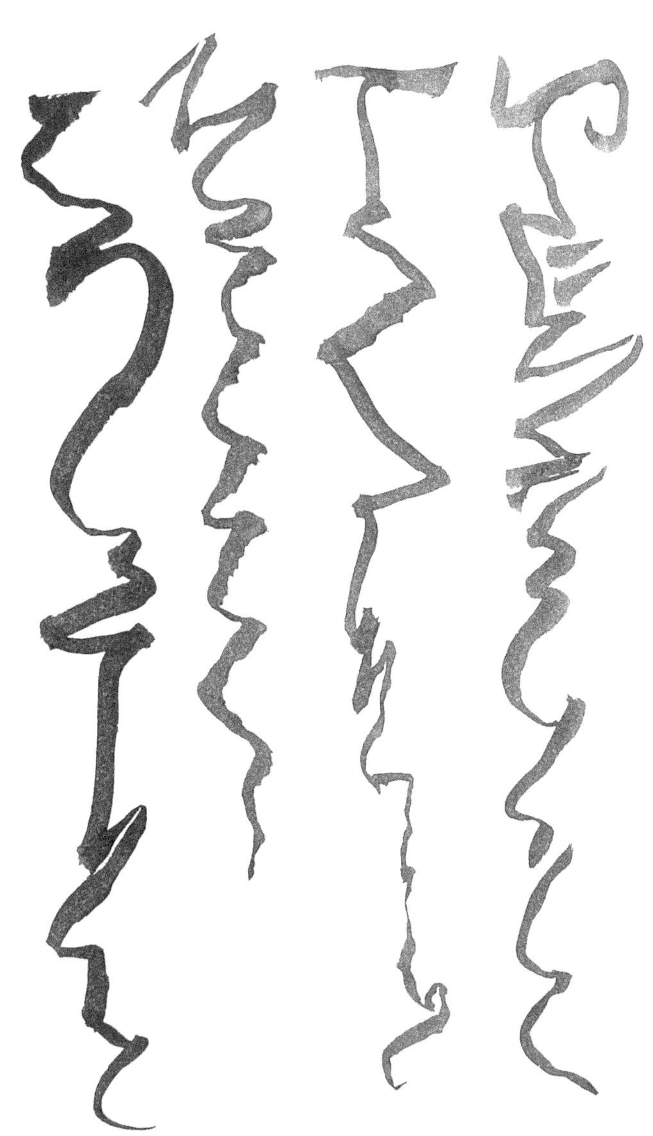

QUI

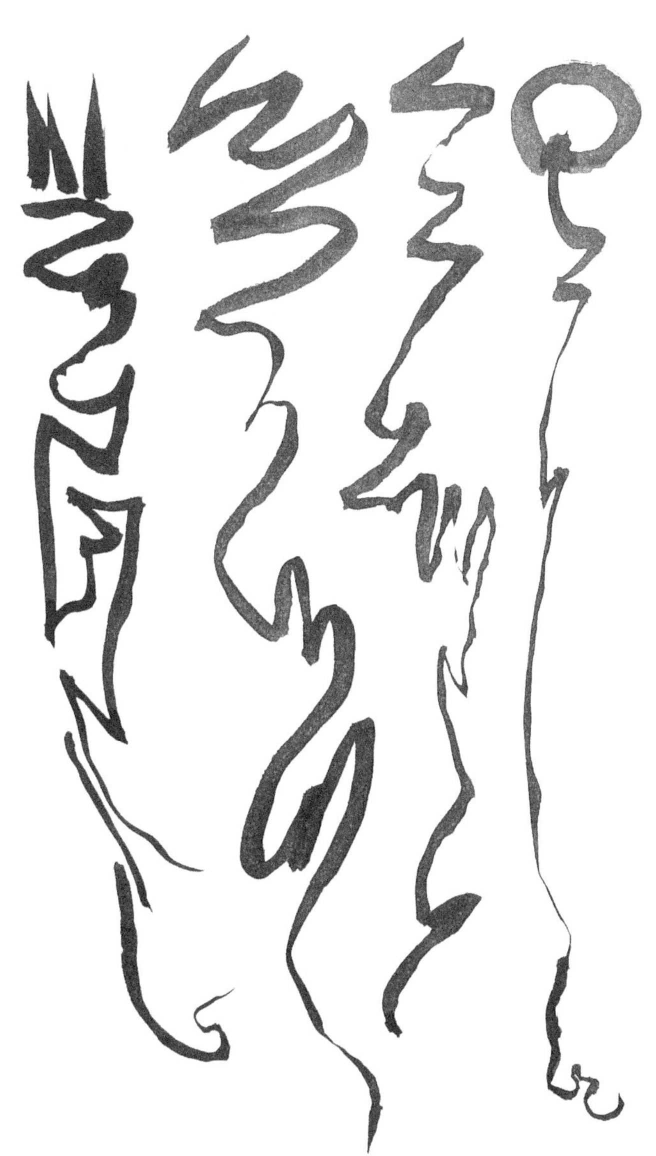

TE

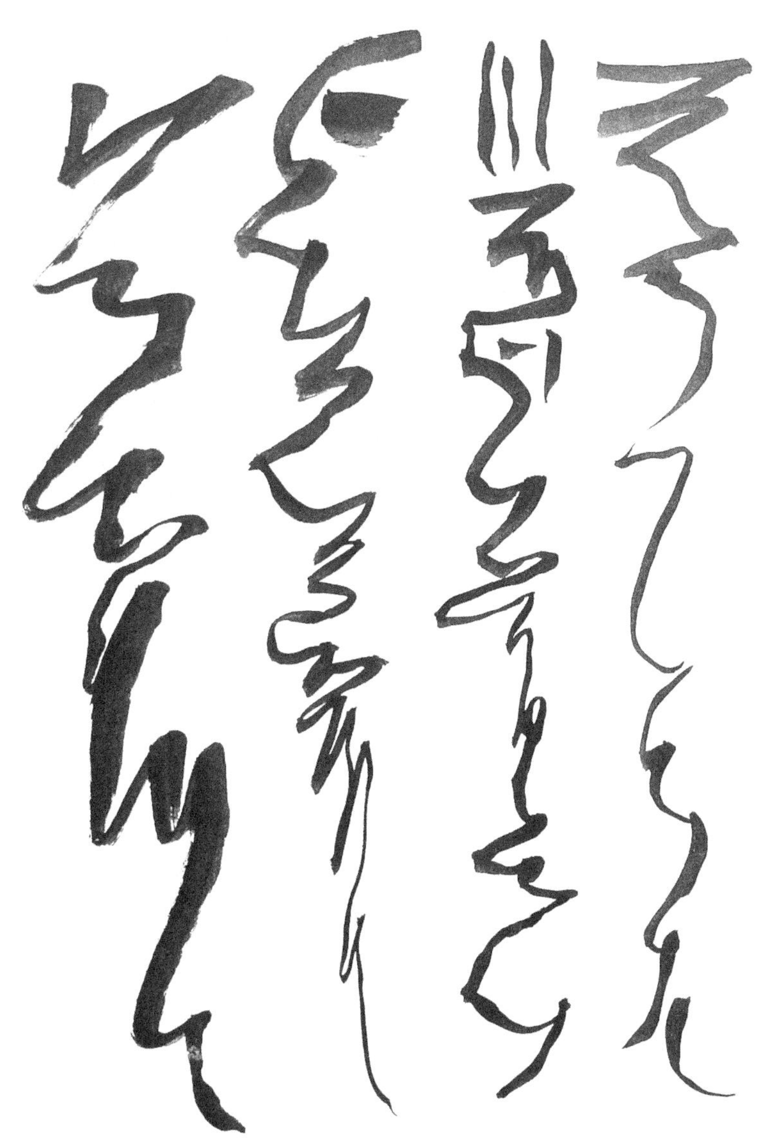

RETIENNENT

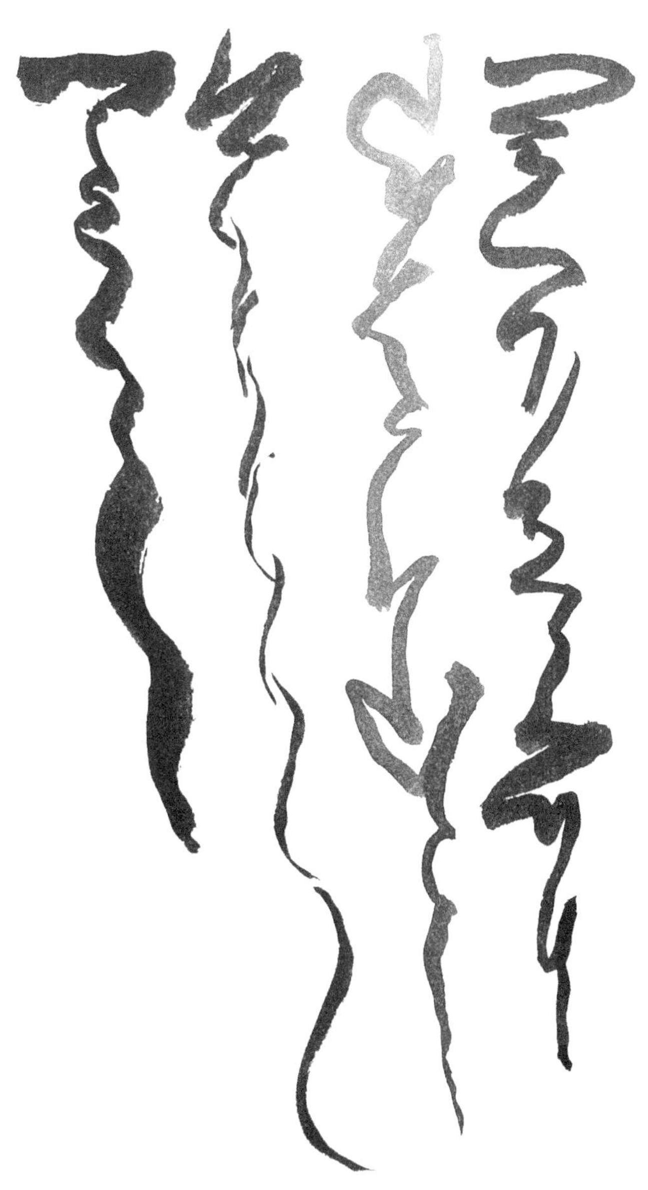

EN

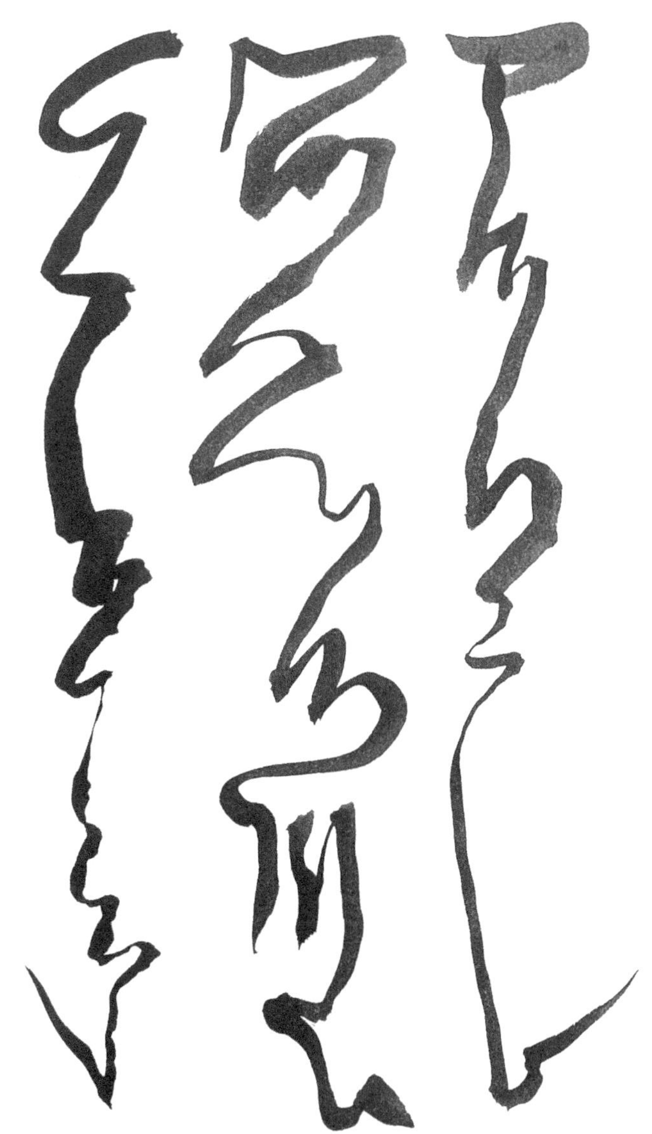

HAUT

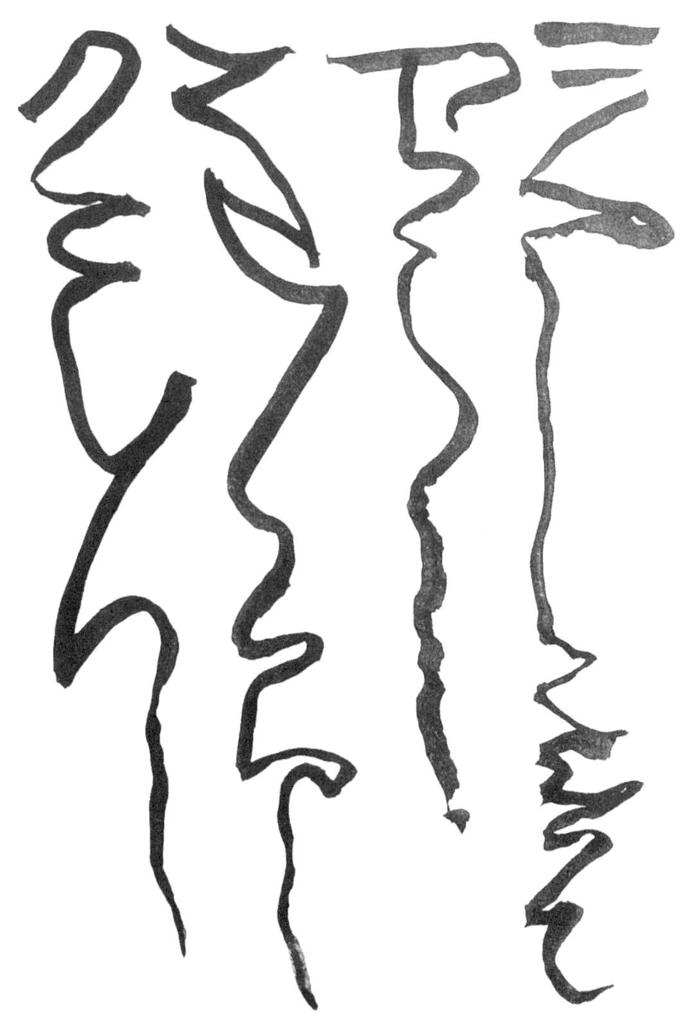

ET

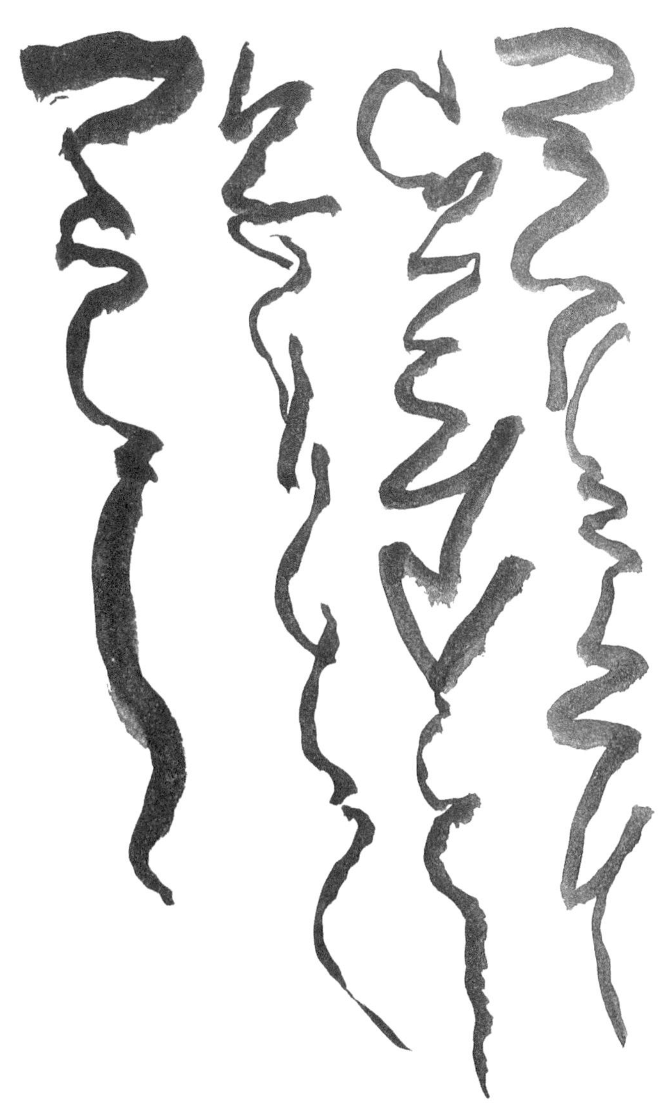

EN

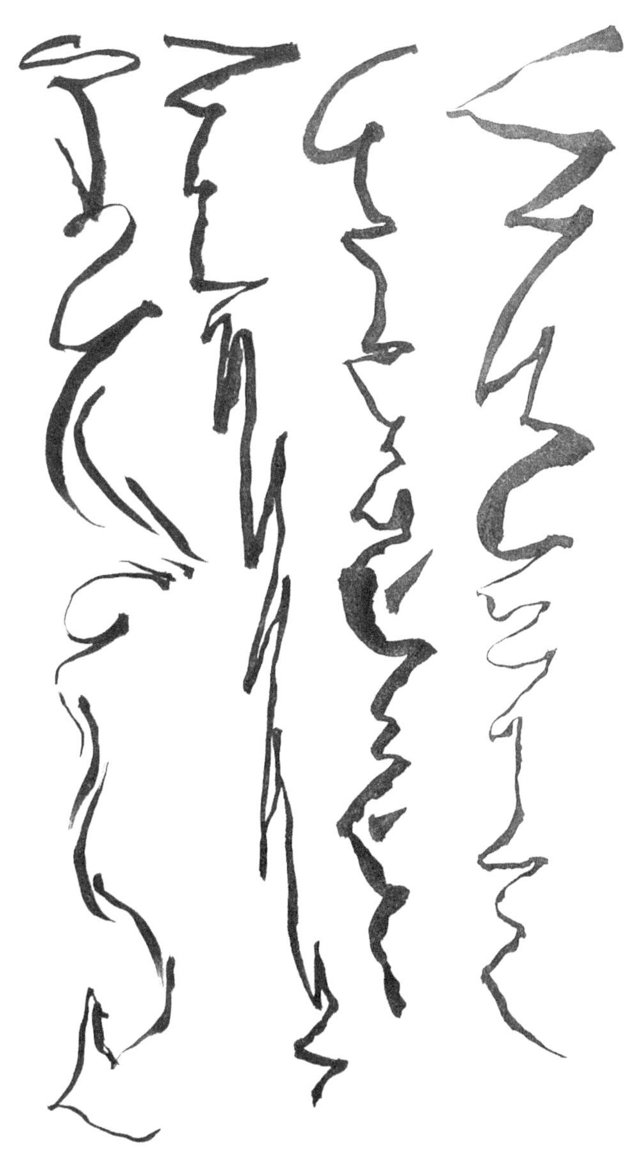

BAS

AUTHOR'S NOTE

The writing was inspired by Japanese Drunken Script (*shodō*) utilizing fragments of characters from various Drunken (cursive) scripts, Japanese and Chinese (semi-cursive) calligraphy, Persian calligraphy, ligatures, glyphs, print ornaments and numerous forms seen while strolling.

The writing was done Hitsuzendō-like style with a single brush using sumi-e ink on Arches Satiné watercolour paper.

The name of my writing style is Laughing Raven (笑うレイヴン).

COLOPHON

The front cover image was generously allowed by Peter James (@ambientabbot).

Mary Frances (@maryfrancesness) graciously allowed the image used for the back cover.

The quote as Preface was found in an article in Wikipedia.

Abaddon was used for the front cover, half-title and title pages.

Asset was used for the single words expressed.

Bodoni Ornaments and Blue Goblet Ornaments were used.

Charlamagne STD was used for the dedication and on the back cover.

IM FELL Fench Canon PRO was used for the common text.

Rackham was used in different places.

www.ingramcontent.com/pod-product-compliance
Lightning Source LLC
LaVergne TN
LVHW020510100826
845148LV00003B/749

* 9 7 8 1 7 3 5 2 7 0 7 6 0 *